Love, Death, the Cosmos, and the Kitchen Sink

Also by Terry Deague
The Spaceman
Where Pademelons Play

Love, Death, the Cosmos, and the Kitchen Sink

Terry Deague

First published in 2025 in Melbourne, Australia

Copyright © Terry Deague 2025

The moral rights of the author have been asserted.

All rights reserved. Except as permitted under the Australian Copyright Act 1968 (for example, a fair dealing for the purposes of study, research, criticism or review). No part of this book may be reproduced, stored in a retrieval system communicated or transmitted in any form or by any means without prior written permission.

This publication is a work of fiction. All characters and places, other than those clearly in the public domain, are fictitious and any resemblance to real persons, living or dead, is purely coincidental.

Typeset and printed in Australia by BookPOD

ISBN: 978-0-6484287-4-9 (pbk) ISBN: 978-0-6484287-5-6 (e-book)

A catalogue record for this book is available from the National Library of Australia

I don't know what to tell you about.
Death or love? Or is it the same thing.

Svetlana Alexievich

Contents

Foreword ix

My Life Pre-COVID 1

COVID and Associated Privations 79

My Life Presumed Post-COVID 197

Afterword 291

Acknowledgements 293

About the Author 295

Foreword

You have my permission to regard this compilation as my take on *Love, Death, etc.* as promised in its eponymous title-page, and as I perceived such matters from 2019 to 2024. I took the trouble to record each individual perception as it came to me as a blog on my webpage (**https://terrydeague.com**). So, *in toto*, these blogs are a form of personal diary covering this period of my life, a diary of my musings, my misgivings, and sometimes of my most defining experiences. It is a diary that, since its inception, has been open to the world at large, and I like to think read by a few of its inhabitants.

I have organized my compilation into three somewhat artificial sections that embrace those challenging years of the COVID pandemic. I have labelled these sections *My Life Pre-COVID*, *COVID and Associated Privations*, and *My Life Presumed Post-COVID*. As you might expect, the sections run seamlessly into each other as parts of the same story always should.

I confess that, for the purposes of this compilation, I have treated my blogs as if they were first drafts, and have taken the liberty of making what I consider to be significant improvements to them before anthologizing them. Will you forgive me on this score? Please indulge my fetish and let me aspire to perfection if I so choose. I promise I'll not pursue perfection to the extent it becomes the enemy of the good.

My scientific background, evident in both my qualifications and my experience, necessarily informs what I write. How could it be otherwise? One might generally suppose my major treatise to the world to be my Ph.D. in nuclear physics from the University of Melbourne but, on the grounds of the breadth of knowledge I have acquired in the field of physics (and I fancy in many other fields besides), I have taken yet another liberty: that of commenting with impunity on matters outside of my specialty. Do I seem arrogant? Am I up myself? I'd maintain that all of us who have lived in this world for a time, and have been halfway curious about the way it works, are entitled to be both specialists and generalists.

The accidental death, in October 2023, of my beloved partner, Janet Ward, of more than thirty three years standing, had the effect of rendering me pretty well incapable of any sensible action, an effect I insist was wholly proportionate to the incomprehensible loss I was now destined to endure. I was well into my third novel up to this point but, subsequent to my tragic bereavement, found I lacked the power of intense application necessary to continue with a project of such moment. Janet, my anchor while I wrote, was no longer available to me for this (or indeed for any) purpose. To my chagrin, accompanied by blackest disappointment, I found that nor was *I* available to *her* for any purpose.

I'm confident the power to write novels will return to me in time but, in the interim, I'm embarking on what I assume to be this less demanding venture, one that I hope shall be no less engaging to readers, and that could have the added advantage of being cathartic for me.

The least I can do is dedicate my efforts in this regard to the memory of Janet, which I now do.

My Life
Pre-COVID

20 January 2019

There Be Pademelons …

I have just finished my first novel, Where Pademelons Play, and published it independently. You will find some details on my webpage, **https://terrydeague.com**, which I hope might encourage you to buy a copy.

For your benefit, I reproduce the blurb on the back cover of my book, which I trust encapsulates the main drift of the novel:

> *'If the dead only knew, they would spin in their graves.'*
>
> *But what if the dead are not to be found in graves at all, but in a world beyond graves, from where they could exercise omnipotent powers to investigate the circumstances of their deaths?*
>
> *The late Mark E Larker. fashion photographer is a case in point. When he exercises his powers in this way, he finds the circumstances of his death to be less than kosher. One Harry McMinn, techno-nerd, is heavily implicated. From his*

> *privileged viewpoint, Mark tracks Harry's life, presenting its narrative to his fellows in the afterlife, whom he refers to affectionately as 'pademelons', aka small wallabies. Denizens of the afterlife find presentations such as these, especially when spiced up with lively theatrics, to be useful diversions from the extreme boredom of eternity.*
>
> *Harry's life, so presented, moves from birth, through an angst-filled adolescence, through lucky dealings in business and in personal relationships, through entanglements with international crime syndicates, and through numerous brushes with death. Harry comes out of it all smelling of roses, ready and willing to go on from strength to strength. The same cannot always be said of Harry's talented circle of friends. Most come to grief. One of this circle, Mark, dies at the hands of the criminals.*
>
> *Mark resigns himself to the discovery that fortune in earthly life is unfairly distributed. He settles back to make the most of the eternity, too terrible to contemplate, that awaits him.*

Does that whet your appetite? Then buy my book.

A few aficionados seem to want to know how an author goes about writing a work of fiction. Why they would want to penetrate these black arts is beyond me. But I shall oblige them. Be warned. Not every writer's *modus operandi* will be the same as mine. There are probably as many such *modi* as there are authors.

Where Pademelons Play took me about five years to write, excusing the odd bit of dabbling done prior to this. I started with the embryonic idea that events in life happen more by chance than by human design.

So I began at the beginning and kept going. I do not suffer from writers' block for one very good reason: I never imagine what I write will be final. I might write stuff for a few days, let my mind churn for several more days, and then edit heavily. I have no regrets about jettisoned material. Easy come, easy go. I don't sweat the stuff I have rejected.

Rigid plans on paper do not work for me. In the course of writing, I might sometimes stop and jot down a handful of bullet points as a guide to what I should do next. As often as not I will ignore these points, because the stuff going on in my head is more important than them. The points merely serve to jolt my recalcitrant mind into action.

I actively seek things that will jolt my recalcitrant mind in this way. Some things that work for me in this regard are: reading published fiction by other people, walking on the beach, listening to music, and relaxing on my chaise in the company of my partner Janet and with a drink.

Having finished WPP, I find myself at a loose end. I miss my characters as if they were real people. I even fell in love with one of my female characters. Read the book and see if you can guess which one.

I miss them so very much. I may just have to write another novel.

11 February 2019

Life as a Casino

It's hardly an original thought, but I have often felt events in our lives are governed more by chance than by our own design. This is the main thrust of my book, *Where Pademelons Play*.

Take my own life as an example. A science nerd at secondary school in Melbourne, I believed that a career probing one of the deepest mysteries of the universe would be my destiny. So I became a nuclear physicist. Having achieved this somewhat esoteric distinction without successfully shaking down the world (as opposed to Einstein, Heisenberg, or Hawking, guys who really *did* shake down the world), I found the only place I could continue my studies post-Ph.D. was Saskatoon.

Saskatoon? Now there's a roll of the dice. Does anybody even know where the hell that is?

So fate (not me, God forbid, and not God either) determined I should change fields. In 1972, I moved from Melbourne to Newcastle, New South Wales, to become a researcher in the field of fuel technology with BHP. Sadly, the research laboratory does not exist anymore. Newcastle, which back then was almost synonymous with BHP, is now a much more diverse place, and so much better for it.

In my role there as Research Scientist, I became aware, among other things, of an emerging problem for the inhabitants of the planet. More and more CO_2 was being released into the atmosphere as more and more fossil fuel was being burnt. Many researchers believed this would heat up the planet, so I investigated further, writing a definitive review paper in the process. Back then, there wasn't enough evidence one way or the other, but holy dooley, there certainly is now.

In consideration of the education of my children and, in particular, of my eldest, Jenny, I applied for a transfer back to Melbourne. It was granted.

At this point, chance (with the help of a few bad players among my associates) determined my career with BHP should come to an ignominious end. As did my marriage. I taught high school for a while, until chance (in the form of my partner Janet) determined I should move to a tiny village called Keppel Sands in Queensland and ultimately retire there. Was it chance, then, or me that decided I should go on to write a novel on the influence of chance on our lives?

So, after a five year gestation period, I came up with the final product. *Where Pademelons Play*. It was something I really enjoyed doing. Really. So read it. Enjoy it. As I did. It may help you decide what it is that governs *your* life.

If it's chance that governs it, then I recommend you just go along for the ride. You may, in any case, have no choice in the matter.

And there's a good chance it will be a wild and interesting ride. Life's like that.

28 February 2019

Me and Janet in Taiwan

This photo was taken at a point on the breathtaking east coast of Taiwan, the much less populated side of the contentious island.

It was taken near the small but charming city of Hualien and the spectacular Toroko Gorge, notorious for (pun unintended) gorgeous scenery and falling rocks. A beautiful but dangerous place. Along one narrow track I walked, signs warn you to move on, because rocks surrounding you on top and sides may decide to assert their weighty authority and you may end up being pulped beneath them. But where the hell are you supposed to move on to? One place on the track is as hazardous as the next. There are rocks threatening to fall above and beside you at all points on the track, and plenty of seismic activity encouraging them to do so. The ubiquitous warning signs are clear about this. This is a dangerous place.

I bit the bullet and took the walk anyway. On my own. Taking the danger together with the delight. Janet, wise owl, chose not to.

I survived, and now I may tell the tale.

We love travel. It thills the senses, and feeds the appetite for more, thereby fostering a lifetime addiction. And, supposedly, it broadens the mind.

But does it? That could depend on whose mind.

If the owner of that mind is on the other end of a selfie stick, and is hell bent on nothing more than capturing photographic evidence of his/her presence at the bucket-listed foreign location in question, and then to send such evidence proudly to the folks back home before moving *post haste* to the next location, then it's doubtful such a mind can be broadened by travel or by any other means. The owner of that mind would be better staying home, thereby saving some money, and devoting his/her time to, say, gardening or collecting stamps. Or indulge in the homespun pleasures of the men's shed/gossip group. Or play erotic games with obliging cousins. Always taking comfort from the fact that English shall be spoken wherever he/she should stray.

Conversely, if that mind is Janet's, it will be striving – with a social worker's impulses – to figure out what the people around her think about living where they do. What are the pros and cons of existence in their little patch of earth? What are their traditional values and how do they differ from her own? My mind will be doing something similar, but in a much less systematic way.

Come evening, and we can learn much in the restaurants and

bars of Hualien. But, surely you may ask, there is a language problem? We don't speak their lingo, and they don't speak ours.

You may be surprised how many people abroad speak some English or are keen to learn. And, if we've done our homework, we will have made ourselves familiar with a few stock phrases in *their* first language. You may say that is tokenism, but people are usually flattered that you've taken the trouble.

And, if it comes to the crunch, you can always resort to sign language. That's always heaps of fun for both parties.

11 March 2019

Dreams that Follow You

Earlier this year, I was watching Leigh Sales on ABC 7:30. She was interviewing a person called Layne Beachley, apparently a surfing legend in Australia. Because surfing is not my bag, I was not paying full attention. Then Layne said something that startled me. She said, 'You should always follow your dreams, because your dreams will always follow you.'

B'Jesus! I thought. How cool is that advice. *You can't escape because your dreams will follow you.*

My earliest dream, even before I reached double figures in age, was to tell stories I had made up. If I didn't have an audience, I told the stories to myself. Mouthing them for my own ears.

I am now older, and this same dream has followed (and caught up with) me. I tell stories as before, but these days I write them down.

But that's such a big jump in time. Let's look first at what happened during those intervening years between my childhood babblings and my later-life scribblings.

Because I was good at it, I pursued a career in science and technology. Bursting to solve the mysteries of the universe (in the footsteps of the giants), I embarked on a Ph.D. in nuclear physics at the University of Melbourne. Of course, things turned out to be more mundane than my vain idealism would wish.

As I mentioned in an earlier blog, the only place I could continue to do nuclear physics post-doc was Saskatoon. I hear you ask, Where the hell's that? I'll tell you. It's the bloody end of the earth. If you want more detail, please admit your geographic deficiencies by consulting Google maps or some such.

To stay safe (and warm) in Australia, I changed fields. My research was now in fuel technology for BHP, mostly in Newcastle in New South Wales. It was the 1970s.

An oddity came to my attention out of left field. Researchers round the world were suggesting that the CO_2 released when fossil fuels were burnt might be warming the atmosphere of the planet and that this effect might get badly out of control. I reviewed the research and wrote a review paper. It was well received. It even got a citation in *New Scientist*. I concluded that, with only about fifteen years of reliable data available about the past, it was difficult to draw any conclusions one way or the other about the future. However, as we moved forward, we needed to watch the situation closely. Those pesky boffins might be right, and the situation might become dire.

Now, late in the 2010s, with more than sixty years of reliable data available about the past, and with the development of some spectacular new techniques such as the study of Antarctic ice cores, it is evident that we must act quickly and decisively if our grandchildren, or even our children, are not to be overrun by catastrophic global warming. We must stop using fossil fuels as a power source, as a means of transport, or for any *other* fool purpose. On this issue, the science is adamant.

So. To my dream …

Living now in retirement on the coast in central Queensland, I have changed fields once more. I have written and published a work of fiction. So I am telling stories again. But this time I'm not mouthing them for my own ears. I'm putting them into print for everyone else's eyes. My first novel, which I prefer to call 'a presentation', is called *Where Pademelons Play*. You can find more about it (and buy it!) by visiting my website: **https://terrydeague.com.**

A pademelon is an Australian marsupial, smaller than a wallaby. Something like the Western Australian quokka. But, in my work of fiction, what it represents is somewhat more than its reality on the ground. A pademelon is an omniscient observer in the afterlife presenting stories about real people in the real world.

As author, I find myself fretting for the real-world characters I have created as they negotiate the convolutions of the plot development I have devised for them. I identify with them, love them, laugh with them, and cry for them. I hope my readers can relate to them in similar fashion, because this is how things should happen with all good stories.

I loved writing this novel … oops … presentation. It has given meaning to my retirement years. My future projects, I hope, will continue to do this for me in perpetuity.

Janet, my life partner, has been great in her support. She has gifted me the two most precious things a writer could want: time and space.

And, by the way, her dream caught up with her too. She had always dreamed of being an architect, but foolishly allowed herself to be dissuaded by her school on the grounds only men should choose architecture as a career. So, she became a social worker instead, and a very good one. Then, in retirement, aware now of the error of her earlier ways, she got to design the beautiful house we now live in.

Thank you, Layne. You were right. If my and Janet's experiences are anything to go by, it would appear your dreams do follow you.

13 March 2019

The Midwest Book Review

 **THE MIDWEST BOOK REVIEW**

JAMES A. COX
Editor-in-Chief
mwbookrevw@aol.com
http://www.midwestbookreview.com

278 Orchard Drive
Oregon WI 53575
(608) 835-7937
mbr@execpc.com

Here is one of the more interesting reviews *Where Pademelons Play* has received. OMG, from far away Wisconsin. The world really is a global village.

Wisconsin, I believe, is on the Great Lakes. Isn't it one of those places where, in winter, they cut a hole in the ice, and cast their fishing lines into the frigid water?

> Where Pademelons Play
> Terry Deague
> Privately Published
> 9780648428701 $24.99 pbk / $9.99 Kindle amazon.com
> http://www.midwestbookreview.com/sbw/mar_19.htm
>
> **Critique:** Where Pademelons Play: A Presentation presents a unique take on the afterlife, as a bleak, eternal existence where there are few diversions other than observing, recounting, and performing events from the living world. One such intricate narrative follows a man with the luck of the Devil – or perhaps a talent for stealing good fortune from others who cross his path. Wry, satirical, and sharp-minded, Where Pademelons Play is darkly engaging

to the very last page. Highly recommended, especially for connoisseurs of the macabre fantastic! It should be noted for personal reading lists that Where Pademelons Play is also available in a Kindle edition ($9.99).

I'd be inclined to accept that one. Thanks, Wisconsin. May the yield from your fishing holes prove to be prolific.

25 March 2019

Geography: The Small Picture

Writers are (fancifully) supposed to write (and starve) in garrets, which I believe are poky uncomfortable rooms just underneath the roofs of houses. Dark and dank, they are all the better for writing and starving in. A garret might be all you can expect if you rely on making a living from your writing alone. Garrets are for people without a day job or other independent means.

In my case, the geography is a little more generous, if not in extent then certainly in outlook and degree of comfort. Most of my writing is done from an old fashioned bamboo chaise, held together strategically by lavish amounts of twine. Its location is the verandah of my house, bathed in open air and lit by reflected sunlight. Shrubbery is all around me, its tendrils always threatening to invade.

Nobody who has not sat in one, nursing perhaps a campari and soda in season, can know how comfortable these old chaises can be. Modern imitations do not cut the mustard. Janet, worried perhaps for my safety, thinks this chaise is beyond its use-by date, and has bought me a couple of these modern substitutes out of metal and hardwood respectively. They just lie there unused. Sorry, Janet. I prefer my old rickety bamboo job.

It is my bower, my shady retreat, my haven. I am invisible here from the world, the street, and even from most parts of the house. I am alone here with nature and my thoughts. The constant and varied bird noises make me wonder if I am perhaps in an aviary.

So, I recline there day upon day, hour upon hour, stabbing at the keyboard of my laptop. No. Unlike Rumplestiltskin, I'm *not* spinning gold yarn, but different kinds of anecdote altogether. They are my literary creations. The one I have finished is called *Where Pademelons Play*, and there's another underway. I dare to hope the world shall marvel at my creations.

Not all my writing happens here. But most does. I take my laptop with me when I travel, and have written parts of *Where Pademelons Play* in places like Perth, Melbourne, and Brisbane, where I have tried, mostly in vain, to find replicas of my bower. I am always happy to get home again, so I can write reclining on a bamboo chaise held together by string.

It is my haven of choice and my geography of preference.

8 April 2019

Geography: The Big Picture

I love to travel. At the time this blog gets posted, I will be in Japan. Travel to foreign parts is always full of surprises, and one hopes most of them will be pleasant.

When writing *Where Pademelons Play*, I drew on my first-hand knowledge of many places and, especially, of three points on the surface of the globe.

First is Melbourne, Australia, where I grew up, and where (in thinly-veiled disguise) most of the action takes place. It is where most of my characters were born.

Second is Petrozavodsk on the bank of Lake Onega in north-western Russia. It can get very, very cold here, as Matt discovers when he pays a visit. It is Elena's birthplace and nemesis. Matt and Elena are principal characters in my novel.

Third is an un-named Malaysian rainforest. It is always hot and steamy in such places, as Harry and Sticks – other principal characters in my work of fiction – discover when they visit. Baharudin – one of my important secondary characters – was born in the vicinity.

May I venture an observation I have made, apropos of the human condition, as a result of my many visits to foreign climes?

Ordinary people everywhere aspire just to keep on living on the patch of turf they occupy and call home. There, they hope to end their life a little more prosperous they when they began it. And they hope their children will have an easier life than theirs.

This, in my experience, is a universal aspiration.

22 April 2019

The S-Word in the 21st Century

I lead a very comfortable life in my lovely home on the central Queensland coast. Many others live just like me. Yet I (and surely those others) are fully aware there are people in the world leading much less comfortable lives. Among the least fortunate of these are the 21st century slaves.

But, you may ask, wasn't slavery abolished a couple of centuries ago? Perhaps names like Wilberforce and Lincoln come to mind. This myth salves our consciences to an extent. We can feel justified in getting on with our comfortable lives without ever having to think about, far less address, the problem.

This is only one of many 21st century myths that serve to sooth us into inaction. Hasn't racism been dealt with? Surely that's a legacy Martin Luther King left us. Anti-semitism? But didn't we defeat Hitler? Environmental degradation? Don't we trot along to the supermarket with our own environmentally-friendly carry-bags?

Let's get back to slavery.

My book, *Where Pademelons Play*, informs you, the reader, of a form of 21st century slavery alive and well in our own country. Yes. Shock. Horror. In our very own Oz, the land of oranges and sunshine!

It is sexual slavery. The players in this dehumanizing game are (more than likely) international criminal syndicates, and their unfortunate victims. One of my principal characters, Elena Rusalkova, uses her wits to sidestep these syndicates and avoid this particular form of slavery. Many of her less clever associates do not.

I have gone to great pains, in my book as such, to avoid preaching on social or environmental issues. This is because I believe preaching can be the kiss of death to art. But that doesn't mean I must put aside preaching altogether. Just not in my novels. Preaching is exactly what I am doing in this blog.

My book is for telling stories. The time and place for the soapbox is blogs. And, even on the soapbox, I feel overreach should be avoided. Overreach has a tendency to turn people off.

Read my book. Read my blog. Have I got the balance right? Decide if, when, and how you might address the scourge of 21st century slavery in our comfortable country.

8 May 2019

A Brief History of Human Awareness of Global Warming, and of the Small Part I Played in It

How did people come to realize global warming was a reality? [I prefer the phrase 'global warming' to its euphemism 'climate change'. The euphemism was coined, I suspect, for political purposes, to make the concept easier to debunk.]

John Tyndall, a scientist in the Victorian era, proved that a greenhouse effect exists, but failed to make any strong connection with CO_2 or with global warming. Other scientists (Arhennius,

Calendar) early in the 20th century made these connections, but thought the effects would only be beneficial.

In 1972, electrochemist John Bockris – who coined the phrase 'hydrogen economy' – warned that global warming was hazardous to life on this planet. Given the scant evidence available at this time, his alarmist message was somewhat of an exaggeration. Scientists, like all of us, are prone to use hype and spin to get their message across.

Bockris' line was that hydrogen should replace fossil fuels in our energy mix because fossil fuels, and the CO_2 they emit on a grand scale, were serious global risks. The hydrogen was to be produced using nuclear energy. Bockris did not consider renewable energy was yet up to the task. The *quid pro quo* was that nuclear might not stack up from the environmental and/or safety viewpoints. Nobody would want it in their backyard. Its by-products are the Devil's own work, incompatible with human life. But nuclear is and was certainly a proven technology.

I played a small part in this drama around the time Bockris made his pitch. I wrote a review paper concluding that we should continue to gather evidence because the world could not afford to get this one wrong. For the time being, however, we should stick with fossil fuels rather than go over to the demon nuclear on a grand scale.

Things have changed. There is now more than enough evidence showing fossil fuels to be a fatal choice for this planet. Renewable energy with battery storage now has an advantage over fossil fuels in an increasing number of sectors of our economic life. And there has been a succession of major major nuclear accidents.

The global warming deniers no longer have a case. *Post haste*, we must make the transition from fossil fuels to renewables and embrace a hydrogen economy. There are pathways for Australia to export hydrogen just like it now exports coal. And if loss of Australian jobs is considered the problem, bear in mind the number of jobs that would be created by constructing and running renewables infrastructure and hydrogen plants on our soil.

It's a no-brainer.

Beware the Orang-Utan Spits ...

... and she was.

28 May 2019

A Beautiful Accident

Sometimes beauty happens by accident.

Now, in order for such an accident to happen, there has to be some incipient beauty on which the accident can work its magic. Accident can't change ugliness into beauty. Remember the adage about silk purses and sow's ears. The incipient beauty in the photograph comes from two places. One is the beautiful subject, my beloved life partner, Janet. And the other is the beautiful setting, the bank of the Eure River in Chartres, France.

It is quite some time since I took this snap. In its original form it was an analogue negative taken with Kodak film. Or was it Agfa? These two brand names have been buried so long and deep in the turf of irrelevancy their bones are now fossils awaiting discovery by some future palaeontologist.

I am a very ordinary photographer at best. I might take hundreds of photos before one that is half-way good turns up. Like the above. The end result you see here is a very special accident. The scanning and digitizing process seems somehow to have enhanced its beauty, lending it a hazy impressionist charm. Even the plastic carry-bag does not jar.

It is now an object of accidental beauty. Somehow I created it.

Weather permitting, it is almost *de rigueur* when in French cities, or even in the provinces, to picnic in parks, in street settings, or on long distance trains, with exquisite victuals from a local delicatessen together with a baguette and a bottle of *vin ordinaire*. This custom, pursued with appropriate decorum, is one of the unique charms of France, and is a thing of great beauty in its own right. We indulged in this ritual quite unselfconsciously at lunch time in Chartres that day with nobody batting an eyelid, but with plenty of looks cast in our direction indicating approval and envy. Afterwards, it was so very natural to lie down by the river bank as Janet did in the photograph of my creation.

[No, she hadn't had too much *vin ordinaire*. Janet knows how to hold her liquor.]

Not all creations exude beauty or are accidental. Take the painting *Guernica* by Pablo Picasso for example. It was no accident. And beauty is the last word that springs to mind in its favour. Great work of art it may be, but Picasso's choice of subject is grotesque.

Take another example: George Eliot's novel *Middlemarch*. Assuredly, it is a creation, and a good one at that. But its beauty depends very much on the eye of the beholder, and a tome such as this could never be described as accidental.

So, if they can't be beautiful, what is their point? I believe that many creations, including these two examples I have plucked out of the air, are in the business of providing insight into the way the world works, with a view to informing us on how we may best conduct our lives, sometimes by negative example.

If I may say so, my inaugural literary effort, *Where Pademelons Play*, falls into this category. I'll let you be the judge of its beauty. As for 'accidental', five years of deliberation went into the design of its plot and characters. But I think the final product conveys the idea of a world whose workings are substantially random, together with an infectious optimism that makes it suitable as a model for spirited, if chaotic, living.

Where my eye beholds beauty is not so much in my novel but in the accidental photograph of Janet on the river bank. My eye is not deceived. There lies beauty.

28 June 2019

… and You Thought Skateboarding Was a Dangerous Activity!

This is a group of *Awa Odori* dancers from the city of Tokushima in Japan. In August every year, they participate in the biggest, most important, and most spectacular dance festival in Japan. It takes over the otherwise sleepy streets of the city completely. The population of Tokushima effectively doubles during the festival.

Even though I have been to Japan more times than I can remember, I regret I have never attended the festival. Fortunately, a troupe of *Awa Odori* dancers perform some of the more distinctive routines just about every day of the year at an indoor location in Tokushima. I have seen their performance a couple of times.

They are amazing.

[Is the general public invited to join in? Yes, even round-eyes are. I have been invited, and given no option but to accept.]

Awa Odori is not a complex dance. But it is distinctive. Its mix of costumes, colour, exuberance, synchronicity, and elemental music make it a hypnotic experience when observed. Adaptations of the style of *Awa Odori* keep cropping up all over the shop in places outside Tokushima. Imitation is indeed the sincerest form of flattery.

The dance relates to the centuries-old Japanese tradition of *Obon*, whereby dead ancestors return to earth to see how their descendants are getting on. *Obon*, which happens throughout Japan in August, is a happy time, essentially a welcoming ceremony for the returning dead. It is party time. It involves, among other things, vigorous group dancing. *Awa Odori* is the most famous of these dances.

The concept of the returning dead seems irresistible and pervasive across all cultures. Though we are bound to agree it is in no way supported by science, we all nonetheless choose to entertain such an idea to some degree or other. It is a comfortable prop for us, in the same way religion can be.

I use hauntings of precisely this stripe to frame the fictional story of Harry McMinn in my book, *Where Pademelons Play*. The pademelons in my story are nothing more nor less than the returning dead in proxy.

Many Japanese art forms are culture specific, and tend to resist transfer to other cultures. In this respect, they seem to exemplify the shoguns' policy of *sakoku* in the 17th and 18th centuries when Japan was effectively a closed society. *Kabuki*, *Noh*, and perhaps *haiku* are examples of such art forms.

But *Awa Odori*, and its attendant notion of the returning dead, is definitely an exception. Dance is a universal language.

There are other exceptions. To mention a few: woodblock prints of the likes of Hokusai, Utamaro, etc., the novels of Haruki Murakami such as *Norwegian Wood*, *The Wind-Up Bird Chronicle*, etc., films from *Rashomon* to *Departures*; and much more besides. Sushi, beer, and sake also travel very well indeed. I'm sure you must have noticed.

We should cherish the culture that gave us (among many other things) the *Awi Odori* dancers. And perhaps we could try to understand those other Japanese art forms that are a little less accessible to us. You never know what you might be missing.

22 August 2019 (and revisited on 7 April 2022)

Death with Distinction

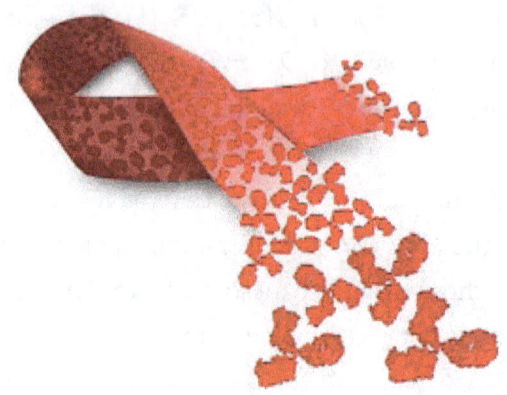

June (not her real name) was one of several women I pursued around that time early in my life when I really didn't have a clue how to engage effectively in such pursuit. I knew what heterosexual relationships had to offer, I knew I was desperate to take advantage of that offer, but I didn't have any inkling of how to close on such advantage. I wanted an instruction manual, or better still a private tutor. When women sensed this, they wanted out. Who could blame them?

To this day, I have a fair recollection of June's face. Where possible, when describing a face, I like to refer to that of some public figure or celebrity with which it may be compared. But in June's case, I can find no obvious comparison.

She would not have been regarded as a beauty. For starters, her nose was too dominant and her cheeks too chubby. Her figure was well-rounded, but her stature short. She had mouse-brown hair and (I think) eyes of a similar colour. She used little or no make-up. She made minimal effort to dress to advantage. With June, you got what you saw. So, you might ask, where was the allure?

Well, her love of life shone through. Her eyes were like cheeky animals seeking always to engage those of other people in boisterous play. A distinctive sense of humour always lurked, often expressing itself via choice verbalisms exclusive to her. For example, in her parlance, people who had lost their cool, were 'fit to can'. Or, she would mock people who were taking themselves too seriously with the exclamation 'Diddums!' I have no idea of the etymology of any of her bespoke expressions.

Though her parents were well-to-do professionals, with a distinct kudos in respectable society, she did not let this affect her choice of friends. She was always prepared to slum it when necessary, e.g. when she took up with me.

With justification, June could be, and often was called, a human dynamo. Her passion was the outdoors and she infected me with this passion. To this day, I have a love of the natural world, for interacting with it, and for the quasi-religious experience it is known to engender. The outdoor locales we explored are, not without justification, often compared to cathedrals. We stood in awe of mountains seeming to connect heaven and earth. We ventured into gorges threatening to close like Gothic arches over our heads. We clambered over rocks as heavy as the Commandments themselves, or as sin if you like. We baptized our sodden walking boots (and ourselves) in clear alpine streams. We mixed it with flora bright and beautiful, and with fauna great and small.

Nature. The old-time religion. Live within it, marvel at it, respect it.

Neither June nor I brought any special talents to bear in this outdoors arena. We tried our hand at a few esoteric sports: snow skiing, water skiing, horse-riding, surfing, and the like. They were just not our bag. Without the capacity to boast of and/or call upon any skilled trades (so to speak), we each settled for the role of unskilled labourer. I talk here of a labour of love. Hiking with full packs, sleeping in small tents, threadneedling rough bush tracks, negotiating near-vertical rock faces, splashing about in icy-cold pools, cooking round a smoky campfire, and the like. Though we loved these simple pleasures with a vengeance, we hadn't the special skills required for conventional displays of excellence. All we had of note was the ability to rough it.

June was a disciplinarian. She made the rules and then enforced them. She took the lead and I followed, entranced by the natural world and enamored of her. These were halcyon days for me. But, of course, they were not to last. As far as relationships were concerned, I was a total klutz and she knew it.

I was devastated when it ended. I had played the main game and lost decisively. But time passed, and wounds healed, albeit slowly.

Many years later, both married now but not to each other, we met up again. We were thankful for the water that had passed under the bridge. We found we were able to relax with each other. The past, another country, fell foul of fickle memory. We related to each other now like old platonic friends. Perhaps brother and sister.

Neither marriage was to last. Hers foundered first. She embarked on a succession of casual relationships, and I lost track of her. The next thing I knew, I was at her funeral.

The church where the service was held was the sort of place everyone who was anyone went to be seen and be seen to be seen. The Anglican priest delivered a predictable eulogy, rattling on about a life well lived but tragically cut short. At age fifty. Afterwards, people huddled in groups and nodded gravely (pun unintended). And I was re-united with June's younger sister, Meredith. Not, of course, her real name.

Meredith in no way resembled June. She liked to inhabit a world where roads were bitumen black, footpaths were firm under the feet, make-up was the standard presenting surface on female faces, and class distinction was enjoined with enthusiasm. She was intelligent, and closer to being a conventional beauty than was June, but hardness wracked her features. The line of her mouth was immobile as if it were stitched onto her face. She could be blunt. She held the view that social niceties such as tact and diplomacy were only necessary should one belong to the lower orders. Straight (and often brutal) talk was the unquestioned prerogative of her class.

Meredith had had the B-word flung in her face more than a few times. I doubt if June had ever had this pleasure.

A week or so after the funeral, Meredith contacted me. She felt she owed it to me to 'bring me up to speed re June', and proposed we meet for lunch at W, a fashionable restaurant in the right part, her part, of town.

She arrived soon after me. Her dress – conservative, expensive, and fashionable – was a one-piece knee-length woolen outfit in deep pink, overhung by a double strand of pearls almost to the region of her navel. Though intended to emphasize a shapely figure, her general presentation could not disguise some untidy rolls of flesh in her midriff region, signs (I guessed) of age and the good life.

After we had placed our orders, she told me, across a white starched tablecloth laid fastidiously with cutlery and napkins, that

June's ashes had been buried besides a waist-high rocky outcrop located on their country property at M. This apparently accorded with June's expressed wish for an unadorned memorial. We both agreed this was in keeping with her love of the natural world.

Our meals arrived. Meredith came to the point. June died of AIDS, she said.

She waited for me to show signs of surprise and/or shock. I certainly felt both, but I doubt I showed either, which may or may not have disappointed her. I waited for her to continue.

She obliged. The thinking at the time, she said, even among professionals, was that AIDS was a gay man's disease. Women didn't catch it. So when June presented to doctors with vague flu-like symptoms that refused to go away, they were clueless. She was passed from specialist to specialist to no avail. Months passed, then years.

One day, Meredith recounted, June was having morning coffee with a female friend. Allison P, she said. You may know her.

I shook my head. Our meals arrived. A Thai salad for me and *coq au vin* for her.

Meredith continued with her account. June asked Allison about an old flame, she said, with whom she'd had a brief affair.

June's affair? I asked.

Meredith nodded, then continued. 'Any news of Ray lately?' June asked. 'Hadn't you heard? He died,' was the reply from Allison. 'How?' asked June. 'AIDS. Ray was bi.'

I drew breath audibly. Jesus, I said, what a ghastly way for June to get the news.

Self diagnosis, said Meredith dispassionately. June went straight back to her doctor and demanded he test her for HIV.

It was all downhill from there, Meredith continued. Near the end, family and friends were taking turns to push her around in a wheelchair. I reflected, What an ignominious end for the super-active person I remember.

A common and garden UTI took her out in the end.

Meredith changed tack. She adopted the patronizing manner she often used with her perceived social inferiors. Her tone was pompous.

Of course, she said, it will come as a complete surprise to the average Joe Blow that nobody actually dies of HIV *per se*. That's not the way the little chappy works. AIDS is a complex of symptoms, not the disease itself. What you die of is an opportunistic infection that takes advantage of your compromised immune system. But I'm sure you knew that.

I saw it as clear as day. June – yes it was June, I swear – put in an unexpected appearance. Tapping the tip of Meredith's nose, she said, Diddums! Then she was gone.

Meredith picked up a chicken drumstick between thumb and forefinger and waved it in the air.

I have it on good authority, she said, that June was the first woman in Australia to die of AIDS. Number one.

Some people will do anything for fame, I quipped.

Meredith munched on her drumstick for a while, before putting it down and continuing her spiel, which took the form of a savage back-handed compliment to me.

I've always imagined, she said, that June would have done much better had she taken up with an ordinary person like you. It would have saved us all a great deal of angst.

Perhaps not surprisingly, that was a conversation stopper. After such a carambole, all that remained for us was to pay for the meal, which I believe we did by splitting the bill. Then, in less time than it takes to say 'human immunodeficiency virus', we were out in the street, and I was bidding farewell to Meredith forever.

On my own now, and dazzled by the bright Australian sun, I made my way slowly along a street lined with *faux* European shopfronts, testament to the Oz cultural cringe. Churning things over in my head, I found myself in conversation with June. Conversation vivid and vital, but taking the form of thought only, without moving lips or vibrating air.

June, I asked, what in the world could you have been thinking? Did you forget that, when riding unfamiliar roads, helmets are always advisable?

Spare me the lecture, was her reply. There's stuff here you can't possibly be party to. And wouldn't even want to.

Try me, I said.

I mean the shock of discovery, then the anguish, then the grief. Finally, my fierce anger against the whole world for the cards it dealt me. What right had my comfortable world to turn on me like this?

You were fit to can? I suggested.

Totally.

Well take my advice, I said. Don't do it again.

Sor-ry. My apologies for being such a stupid pleb.

You're no pleb, I said. No way. *I'm* the ordinary one.

Sure. And I'm so special I died through common and garden stupidity.

It was a first for Australia.

Up yours, squire.

Your death was one of a kind. Death with distinction.

∽

[7 April 2022

Almost three years ago now, and prior to the COVID pandemic, I put together a post about an earlier pandemic that wreaked its havoc back in the 1980s. I mean the HIV (AIDS) pandemic. Though useful comparisons between these two scourges can be made, there is one very important difference between them. At least in the early years, until the development of effective anti-viral drugs, infection with HIV was invariably fatal. A positive HIV diagnosis was a death sentence. It was a scary situation for those of us who lived through these times.

My post was very well received when published back in August 2019. Some people even confessed to being profoundly moved by it. Sensing it may have some increased relevance in these COVID days, I'm re-posting it now, in April 2022, for your benefit. The more pedantic among you may notice some minor changes I have made. Such is an author's prerogative.

Enjoy.]

19 September 2019

My Take on Toni Morrison

Toni Morrison died on 5 August 2019. She was a prominent, perhaps *the* most prominent, African-American novelist in the USA in her day, and Nobel Prizewinner in 1993. Whatever your personal opinion of her written works, you cannot deny her importance in the canon.

Some years ago, I read *Beloved*, arguably her most famous novel. At the time, it had just been made into a film with Oprah Winfrey as its principal. I did not take to the book or to the film. To my mind, there was too much gratuitously supernatural stuff in the story. Also, its style seemed to be derivative to an extent. It borrows heavily from the style of William Faulkner.

I like William Faulkner's writing very much. I think he has

claim to be regarded as the greatest US writer of all time. But to emulate his style successfully is impossible and, to try to do so, is probably fatal.

There will be many people who disagree with my comments about *Beloved*. Some will doubtless be incensed by the adverse judgment I make about their 'beloved' book. But, I ask of them, please don't burn me at the stake. Literature, like all art, is a very personal thing. They are entitled to their opinion and I to mine. I'll respect theirs and hope they'll respect mine.

Now, many years later, I am reading another of Toni Morrison's books: *Song of Solomon*. The reason I am reading it right now is nothing to do with her death. The two events are quite unrelated. I just happened to pick up the book one day and started reading. Currently, I am about half way through it, so I can't give a final verdict yet.

But I haven't yet come across anything outrageously supernatural. And the nod to Faulkner is worrying me a lot less this time. The characters, almost all African-American, are intensely engaging. After a few chapters, I started to feel they could be unlikely neighbours of mine. Some of the dialogue Toni Morrison has written for them is mind-blowing. I am starting to feel I might have to update my view of her body of work. In a positive sense.

Sometimes, first lines in a novel stay with you for ever. Hence Herman Melville's *Call me Ishmae*l. Or Leo Tolstoy's reflections, in *Anna Karenina*, on the subject of happy families. Or, from L P Hartley: *The past is a foreign country. They do things differently there*. Well, the first lines in *Song of Solomon* are pretty memorable too. They go thus: '*The North Carolina Mutual Life Insurance agent promised to fly from Mercy to the other side of Lake Superior at three o'clock.*' Cool.

Back to William Faulkner for a moment. In the 1960s, I plucked from a library shelf the first ever Faulkner novel I was to read. It was *The Mansion*, third in the so-called Snopes trilogy. It introduced me to the fairy-tale world of the deep south, with said fairy-tale being of the extremely Grimm variety. I will never forget the opening sentence: *The jury said 'Guilty' and the judge said 'Life', but he didn't hear them.*

Could you contemplate for a moment putting down a book that started that way?

As for the Toni Morrison book I am currently reading, I may let you know via a future blog what my final verdict is once I have read it through to its final words. I have taken a quick peek at those words. Naughty of me, I know. They seem enigmatic: *If you surrendered to the air, you could ride it.*

3 October 2019
Binna Burra RIP

Early in September this year (2019), bushfires wiped out historic Binna Burra Lodge in the Lamington National Park in Queensland, together with portion of the National Park itself. Look at the photo above. Does this look like something that would burn easily?

Lamington is warm temperate rainforest. It was formed when most of the earth's land mass was contained in the supercontinent we call Gondwana. So Lamington in some shape or form has existed for hundreds of millions of years. That makes it older, arguably, than the dinosaurs. By far. Does this sound like something that would burn easily?

It should not burn easily. But we have managed to burn it.

Who are 'we'? My answer would be humankind in the thrall of unfettered industrial development. Who else?

If we subtract the date the industrial revolution started from today's date, we get around 170 years. That's about how long it took us to learn how to burn something that by its very nature should be unburnable. Something that's been around more-or-less without threat of burning for a factor of 100,000,000 years. To call this a priceless antique would be an outrageous understatement.

I first visited Lamington in the 1970s for one day only, in September I believe, and will remember the impression it made on me until my final moments on this planet. Frequently and quite deliberately, I call up the memory of that day so as to polish it till it gleams, before setting it back in place in some readily retrievable recess of my mind. I treasure that memory.

On that day, I left Binna Burra Lodge for a walk that would take me about six hours return. For most of my journey, the terrain looked like the picture above. I had no specific destination. Each point in my journey was in itself a destination so seductive as to take my breath away. Words, even pictures, cannot convey what I felt. The canopy overhead wrapped round me like a moist green cave, sanctuary from all the bustle of my then life in the big city. Sights to which the above photo can't do complete justice, sounds of birdlife in essential harmony with the environment, smells conveyed on the freshest of fresh air, and the touch of gentle temperature and humidity on my skin, made for a total experience of pure magic.

Six hours later I emerged. Outside, unawares to me, it had been raining. But, within the rainforest itself, the raindrops had been collected as they fell by the thick fleshy leaves of the canopy, turned to invisible vapour, and blended into the benevolent air. I had had no need of an umbrella during my walk.

Does this sound like something that would burn? You might as well try to burn the Great Barrier Reef.

Oops. I do believe we're working on it.

17 October 2019

Three Faces of Ignorance

Education trumps ignorance every time. Universal education, I believe, is the recipe for a happy and prosperous world. Unfortunately, it frequently seems unattainable. Ignorance flourishes despite best intentions.

Ignorance, like education, comes in various shapes and forms. I give examples here of three particular 'faces' of ignorance I have come across in my wanderings. I am sure there are more than just these three. You, surely, have encountered these three faces. And many more besides.

(1) Ruinous Ignorance

Some years ago, I found myself in Walnut Creek, a town in the San Francisco Bay Area of California. It looked and felt prosperous. Though quite some distance from Silicon Valley, it had a similar feel.

On a bustling street corner in the middle of the day, a woman in her thirties was engaged, very publicly, in a knock-down drag-out fight with somebody I assumed to be her boyfriend. Wisely, he left the scene, and left her at a loss. She turned to the nearest person, who happened to be me.

Can you tell me where the closest bar is? she asked.

As it turned out, I was able to oblige. I gave her directions. She heard my accent, and was curious. [I give her full marks for curiosity.]

Where are you from? she asked.

Australia, I said.

Oh, that's in Italy is it?

No, I replied, it's a bit further south.

Oh, in Africa?

No, it's …

But there was no sensible answer I could give. How would you reply to a person who had such a woeful grounding in geography? She headed off to look for the closest bar. I suspected geography – or the lack of it – was not her only problem.

I thought about our encounter, and began to feel pity for her. What hope was there for her? She was adrift. She had no anchor. Or, at best, her anchor was dragging. She was not equipped to cope with an unsympathetic and unforgiving world. She was doomed.

Her ignorance would be her ruin.

(2) Blissful Ignorance

Then there was the time I drove with my partner, Janet, through the Amish country in Eastern Pennsylvania. It was July. Janet was on the look-out for a quilt to buy. Amish women are known for the quality hand-made patchwork quilts they produce.

It was a fine day. On the road we travelled, there was no shortage of quaint farms, cottages, and horse-drawn buggies of the stripe that shouted Amish. Colourful quilts for sale were on display in the front yards of nearly every property.

Janet saw the quilt she liked, and we drove in. The woman, in late middle-age, who had made the quilt, greeted us. She was dressed traditionally and severely in bonnet and ankle-length costume. She was relaxed, serene, and as if transplanted from another age. I shall call her Grace. That was not her real name.

We expressed admiration of the many quilts she had produced. She retrieved the one we wanted. We paid her – by credit card! Then we engaged her in casual conversation. I wouldn't give *her* any marks for curiosity. She did not ask where we were from, but we told her anyway.

Australia, I said. Do you know where that is?

No, Grace replied.

… I was beginning to wonder about Americans in general and their grasp of geography …

It's on the other side of the world, I said. Right now, it's night time there. And winter.

Grace nodded, politely but distantly.

Can you imagine that? I asked.

No, she replied.

So Grace not only lacked curiosity. She lacked imagination.

We left, Janet with the beautiful quilt of her choice tucked under her arm, and both of us with thoughts in our heads to mull over. Grace's world was circumscribed. That patch of flat earth west of Philadelphia was all she knew. But, despite its geographic limitations, and the lack of conceptual breadth it fostered, she was cool with it. She was grounded in it. She was not unhappy. She was not ruined. She was not doomed.

Just blissfully ignorant.

(3) Wilful Ignorance

Many of you, here in Australia, would be familiar with the national broadcaster. The much-loved ABC. Australian Broadcasting Corporation. Perhaps, like me, you tune into it frequently.

I was tuned in one fine afternoon, on my car radio, while driving from Rockhampton to my home in beautiful Keppel Sands. I was listening to a former cabinet minister in a former federal government who, these days, hosts a forum on Auntie. That's the affectionate name many of us have chosen to give the ABC. To show our love. Auntie.

I shall not name the host of this forum. But many of you will have listened to her, and will know *exactly* to whom I refer.

On this particular occasion, she was interviewing the editor of a UK journal often described as 'right wing'. Personally, I dislike this label. It suggests that political standpoints in the 21st century are restricted to a one-dimensional continuum, with 'left' at one end and 'right' at the other, when clearly they are not. Not all viewpoints fall on a single straight line. Mine doesn't, for one.

I would have preferred that the host challenge her guest and vice versa. But this did not happen. There was no element of debate in their discourse. They simply backed up each other's views, with a minimum of substantive argument. They put me in mind of Tweedledum and Tweedledee. Or of Little Sir Echo. In fact I believe, in the trade, the metaphor for this type of forum is 'echo chamber'.

What views were they espousing? That the young climate activist Greta Thunberg should go back to her classroom in Sweden and stop allowing herself to be used by 'adults'. Little or no critique was made of Greta's views. They seemed content instead just to shoot the messenger. And when words such as 'autism', 'used', and 'exploitation' were spat out, and phrases such as '… history of mental health issues …', '… go back to school …', and '… adults know better …' were bandied about, it sounded more like character assassination. Always a very bad look. Health and age should not be issues. Viewpoint, and the substance behind it, should.

I could say many more things, but I shall mention just two.

The ABC audience was told by the echo chamber that Greta should skip her own free time not class time. Now Greta has made clear from the word go that education is pointless if it is offered to someone without a future. What better way is there to make this point than by skipping classes? Her creed is: Do what I do, not what I say.

The ABC audience was also told that 'end of days' scenarios in the past have always turned out to be false. Malthus was given as an example, and I shall help their cause by naming another: Club of Rome. But the present climate emergency is different in a very important respect.

Just a few decades ago, the designation 'climate scientist' did not exist. Now, as we can't help but be aware, the designation absolutely *does* exist, and there are thousands of such scientists around the world. The consensus of virtually all these scientists is that a climate emergency exists with consequences for our planet that are dire.

Neither Malthus nor the Club of Rome had the advantage of a consensus of thousands of researchers. And, without it, they made mistakes, particularly in the timing of their predictions.

Greta has always said 'listen to the scientists'. And she is right. The methodological pillars of modern science are (1) investigation without preconception, (2) an evidence base, and (3) rigorous peer review. This makes their findings as foolproof as findings are able to be in the real world.

A climate emergency is upon us.

I cannot believe host and guest in the forum on ABC are not fully aware of what I say above. And I'm sure they know about shooting the messenger and character assassination. Their's is ignorance by choice.

Wilful ignorance.

The few scientists who oppose what the thousands tell us can be counted in single digits. Yet their voice is so loud it drowns out the consensus view. Why? Because their views invariably get heard in an echo chamber, composed of an army of Little Sir Echos, and endorsed by more powerful forces. Call them Big Sir Echos. Those who conspire in this fashion know full well where the real truth lies. So again, this is wilful ignorance.

There is so much of it about.

7 November 2019

The Exterminating Angel

At a film society screening in the 1970s, I saw a film which blew my brain, almost literally. Not just because it was a superb film (which it was), but because it re-created for me a recurring nightmare from my early childhood. The film, in black-

and-white, and made in 1962 by Spanish director Luis Bunuel, was *The Exterminating Angel*.

As I staggered around in a daze afterwards, I asked myself, How could Bunuel have known about my nightmare of decades earlier? The answer is, of course, he didn't. He was simply elaborating on a universal and timeless tale doubtless lurking in the recesses of all our minds. Which is one reason it packs such a punch. Or did for me, anyway.

If you have been reading my blogs, you would know I am a writer. I have written one novel, *Where Pademelons Play*, a real world story framed in fantasy. So, when seeking a theme for my *second* novel, I didn't have to look far. My nightmare and Bunuel's film contain the timeless tale I need. Once again, a real world story framed in fantasy.

I do *not* intend to plagiarize Bunuel nor anybody else. I do *not* intend to re-write *The Exterminating Angel*. The timeless tale from which I intend to grow my story is not Bunuel's exclusive property, nor is it mine. He didn't invent it, and nor did I. It is out there for anybody who might choose to use it as a springboard for their imagination. As Bunuel did. And I intend to.

Realize please that the story I shall tell bears no resemblance to the one Bunuel told in 1962, except that they both feed off the same timeless tale. Two stories may spring from the same premise, but then go off in completely different directions. I assume you would not regard *Lady Chatterley's Lover* as a clone of *Madame Bovary*, just because they share the same central idea: that of an adulterous woman.

I have written about 25,000 words so far, which is probably about a quarter of what I anticipate I shall need to write. I don't want to reveal any more details at present because I really don't know in which direction it will go. No, I have *not* prepared an outline from woe to go. That is not the way I work. Let me tell you how I *do* work.

I set about writing plot and characters as if for a final draft. If what I have written after a few weeks is, in my own opinion, not adequate as a final draft, I revise what I have written, rejecting material as necessary, adding material as necessary. After multiple revisions, a strange thing happens. My characters themselves take the job of writing out of my metaphoric hands. My *actual* hands work the keyboard, but my characters are responsible for the imaginative aspects of the writing. They seem to jump right out of the computer screen for this purpose. I swear this is what happens.

This is why I'm not going to reveal any more details. I can't. I don't even know them myself.

I would venture to make a couple of suggestions to you.

(1) If you have not already seen *The Exterminating Angel*, you should try to do so. If you *have already* seen it, see it again. If you are fluent in Spanish, that's great. If like me you are not, you shall have to read subtitles.

(2) Read my book, *Where Pademelons Play*. It is good.

(3) Watch for the release of my second book. I can't yet give you its title, because I haven't settled on one yet. It will *not* include the words 'Exterminating' or 'Angel'.

21 November 2019

You Should Be Used to It by Now

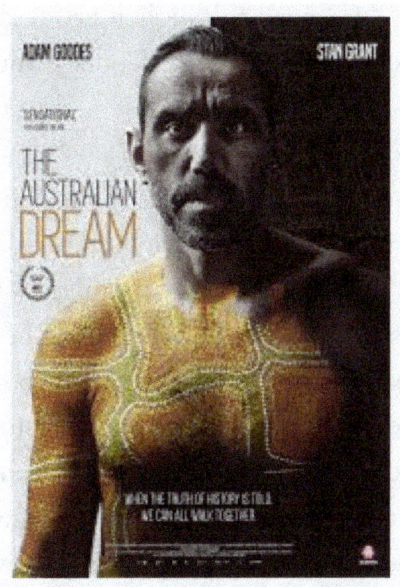

Recently, I saw the Australian documentary film *The Australian Dream* featuring Adam Goodes as himself. My partner, Janet, was moved to tears by the film, and she was not the only one in the audience who was.

For those of you who have been living on Mars, Adam Goodes is a former superstar of Australian Rules Football. The film uses significant events in Goodes' life to make a convincing case for tolerance and against racism in Australia and, by natural extension, elsewhere.

We are all familiar with the xenophobic catch-cry 'Go Back To Where You Came From', used in quite a number of contexts, including (ironically) as unsolicited advice to indigenous

Australians. I would like to add another catch-cry to the pantheon: 'You Should Be Used To It By Now'. It is frequently used when people like Goodes take a stand against racism. The person using it means 'I have the right to express my opinion publicly, so you, the victim of my slurs, need to toughen up.' It is a classic case of blaming the victim. I'm sure Adam Goodes would have heard it said.

Let me give you another example.

Some years back, when the populist politician Pauline Hanson was due to speak in Rockhampton, my partner and I turned out to protest Hanson's objection to Asian immigration, and to Asians generally. We brandished a large white bed-sheet on which was written, 'My beautiful adopted Australian-born half-Chinese daughter was recently told: you should go back to where you came from. Thanks Pauline.' A photograph of the daughter, then aged about 30, was attached. She was Janet's younger daughter, who was adopted by Janet a few weeks after her birth, who was brought up in an Australian environment, and who knows no language other than English.

We hung the bed-sheet on a fence while we went for lunch. When we came back eating our souvlakia, we found two men with shoes and broad-brimmed hats in white, reading our message. They were stereotypes of what was then (and perhaps is even now) known as the 'white shoe brigade'. They were clearly here to support Hanson. When I asked them what they thought of our message, guess what their reply was?

'*She Should Be Used To It By Now.*'

These people certainly know their lines. It's like they are all reading from the same cheat sheet.

I like to think most people in this country are happy to have worthy people like Adam Goodes and Janet's daughter thrive without being subjected to the degree of intolerance I describe above. But there are quite visible and vocal elements in our midst that would shove *their* extreme intolerance down *our* throats. We should push back against these people whenever they raise their ugly heads.

Oh, and … make sure you see the film *The Australian Dream*.

19 December 2019

The Deep North

In 1995, I moved with my partner, Janet, from Melbourne, that big sophisticated city in the south, to Keppel Sands, a small village in Central Queensland. It was to be our new home. This part of Australia is frequently referred to, by those who like to sneer, as The Deep North.

How has it worked out for us?

First, let me tell you a little of its geography and demographics. Keppel Sands is on the edge of the Pacific Ocean, just a tad north of the Tropic of Capricorn. The beach is about a kilometre in length. See the tiny pimple in the photograph at the end of the beach? It is called Musa Head. If you climb to the top of it and then look out to sea, you can count eighteen offshore islands, including the Keppel Group. Then just beyond the horizon is the Great Barrier Reef.

Janet has a twin sister who also lives on a beach on the Pacific Ocean, but on the other (eastern) side of it. Her house is poised uncomfortably on a cliff-edge in a small coastal town called Bolinas in Northern California, overlooking the Farallon Islands. Janet likes to say that if she were to spit on the arc of a great circle, the gob would land on her sister. Don't get me wrong. I believe she loves her sister.

Compared with the gleaming white-sand beaches in the southeast of the State of Queensland, our beach is quite unprepossessing. But it has a couple of advantages. First and foremost few people know about it. If I walk on the sand and find more than about three people there for whatever purpose (walking, swimming, fishing), I find myself asking, What are those people doing on *my* beach?

And it has four-metre tides. This makes it a poor proposition for developers wanting to build canal estates. Nobody wants to get up in the morning to find their boat four metres up or four metres down.

Keppel Sands has only 212 houses, so it is a *very* small village. It has a pub, a school with 2 classrooms, a post office, a shop, and … the Ko-Op. The Ko-Op is, for the most part, a restaurant. Tammy, the chef, has (I am lead to believe) worked at reputable venues in London and Paris. So her meals are almost always good. She puts a lot of imagination into menu design. Her Saturday night specials have become an institution in town. You can look up the Ko-Op on TripAdvisor and see for yourself.

And my book is on sale there. So what's not to like?

Now I don't want to pretend everything about small-village life is hunky dory. There is a tiny coterie of small-minded people in Keppel Sands who seem hell-bent on disruption. Whatever committee it is they join, their only aim is to push themselves forward, to big-note themselves. Making a constructive contribution for the general good is for the birds according to these folk. If lies and fake news are the only way to get attention, they will not hesitate to lie and fake the news. My policy is to avoid these people. They are poison.

The vast majority of folk in Keppel Sands are *not* like this. They are pleasant, supportive, sociable, constructive, and honest. In a big city, you would be hard pressed to find people like this. A former associate of mine, who lived (maybe still does) in a small regional city in Australia, was once asked how he could bear not to live in a big city, thoughtful talented and cultivated person that he was. His response was, 'It's like this. There are twelve interesting people in this town, and I know them all.'

Could big-city dwellers make the same boast?

So the people in Keppel Sands with whom I choose to associate – 'the twelve' so to speak, though there may actually be more – are amenable folk to say the least. They would not hesitate to come to my aid in a crisis, and vice versa. As is the rule in small communities, they know a lot of detail about my private life. How could it be otherwise when we are all at such close quarters? Do they invade my privacy? Do they use this knowledge against me? Of course not. And the *quid pro quo* is I know heaps about *their* private life.

Openness of this kind is the best way to finesse idle or malicious gossip.

I'm not trying to pretend these admirable people don't have

their foibles. Of course they do. They are human. And I'm sure I have foibles too. But I reserve the right not to mention foibles. I'll only mention the good things about them. Why? Isn't the answer obvious? It's because I have to continue to live with them day by day.

Small-village life is not for everyone. For many people, big-city life is their oxygen. But I can honestly say it suits me. And Janet too, I believe. When I left Melbourne a quarter century ago, I was not at all sure I was doing the right thing. Now I am certain.

2 January 2020

When Your Planet Sends You an Eviction Notice ...

Once upon a time it was only those pesky scientists telling us some home truths about climate change. We could brush them off with ease and get on with our lives without having to be bothered by facts and evidence. But now it's not just the scientists telling us. It's the planet we live on. Our landlord, no less.

And the planet is telling us that some parts of its surface are uninhabitable, or about to become so, owing to climate-induced factors such as inundation, drought, or bushfire. It is telling the people who live in these parts they should move on and find somewhere else to live. It is evicting these people, or about to.

What parts are these? Well, for the moment, some small island nations in the South Pacific, like Kiribati. Then parts of California, eastern Australia, and Chile. Then coastal areas of Texas, Louisiana, and Florida. Cities such as Jakarta, Bangkok, New Orleans, and Venice. Beaches such as Miami and the beautiful Stockton Beach in Australia. And unless we do something now, right now, the list will just keep getting longer and longer.

It is happening, just as the scientists said it would. They told us this twenty or thirty years ago, and they were ignored, scoffed at, laughed out of town. But, all along, they were right.

What have the scientists been telling all of us that are prepared to listen? At the risk of sounding like a cracked record, I shall summarize. If you think you have heard this story before, which you certainly should have, please skip the next paragraph.

When we extract, and then burn or otherwise process, fossil fuels – think coal oil and gas – we release greenhouse gases – think CO_2 and methane – into our biosphere. These gases are responsible for the global heating we are seeing. Global heating dramatically increases the chance of all sorts of adverse weather events, like drought, fire, sea level rise, etc. It takes some time for the full-on effect to be realized but, boy, that time is up. We're on the receiving end now.

Denialists are at large, as they always will be. There have been those who denied the earth was round, those who insisted the earth was the centre of the universe, and those who refused to countenance evolution by natural selection. There were people insisting that tobacco does not contribute to premature death, and that no man ever trod on the moon. There are people who reject vaccination because they think it causes autism, and people who don't want to see fluoride added to our water supply.

And now there are people who insist there is no human-induced global heating. All of these people deny science and its evidence base. Recently, some of these denialists have even started to deny they are denialists. To me, that indicates even *they* know their position is on the nose. They want to have their cake and eat it too. How pathetic!

Let's look at some of the tired refrains we are hearing from these incorrigible climate denialists:

(1) "Bushfires have always been with us.' FACT CHECK: Monster bushfires like these ones definitely have *not*. They are a very recent phenomenon. Already, so early in the season, and unfortunately with still more of the season to come, their total extent almost equals that of the all-time record for a season in terms of hectares burnt per annum. Stuff like rain forest that should never in a fit burn *is* burning. You can confirm the assertions I make here by consulting expert opinion, e.g. the Bureau of Meteorology, the Rural Fire Service, and (of course) the people of Australia's first nations.

(2) "We should not indulge in knee-jerk reactions to events.' FACT CHECK: For crying out loud, the scientists have been warning us for decades. This must surely be the longest knee-jerk in recorded history.

(3) 'Scientists shouldn't get into politics.' FACT CHECK: They aren't. For Pete's sake, listen to them. The scientists are getting into science. It's their accusers that are playing politics.

(4) 'We'll meet our Paris target in a gallop.' FACT CHECK: Here in Oz, our target will only be met through a sleazy accounting trick, condemned outright by most of the signatories to the Paris accord. Bad form, Australia!

(5) 'No worries, mate. The firefighters fight fires, because they like doing it.' FACT CHECK: Sure. Just ask any firefighter.
(6) 'God has decided to nail us because we voted for gay marriage.' I won't even dignify this one with a response.
(7) etc, etc, etc.

So, with the denialists denying compulsively, and the planet serving eviction notices willy-nilly, what's in store for us, the meat in the sandwich?

Over thousands of years, humankind has in fits and starts managed to construct a civilization and culture based on evidence, logical thinking, and the ethics of equity. There have been setbacks, some major. Setbacks in the nature of military and colonial adventurism, untrammelled greed, slavery, racial violence, and the like. But generally the better angels of our nature have struggled and won through. Now, however, we face a struggle of a completely different stripe. A struggle to reverse our own adverse impact on the climate. There is no precedent in human history to go by. Are we up to it?

We must disown fossil fuels and embrace renewable sources of energy in their place. The quicker we do this the better. There will be no avoiding blood, sweat, and tears, but the quicker we act the less we will taste of this bitter pill. We owe it to the innocents now. These innocents are our children, our grandchildren, and the multitude of other species with which we share our troposphere. Surely we would wish there to be a place on our planet to take them in.

~

POSTSCRIPT, *New Year's Eve:*

Re my point (1) above:

With fires of unprecedented intensity burning out of control in NSW and Victoria as I type these additional words, the all-time record for hectares burnt per annum must now (for calendar year 2019) have been exceeded. There is a good chance this record will be broken yet again in 2020. These are not statistics to be proud of.

Most people by now will know people, family members or friends, who are affected by the fires to the extent they fear for their homes or even their lives. For example, Janet, my partner, has a daughter in Moruya, NSW, who is cut off in every direction with no way of leaving town.

I am told these fires smell really bad. There is just one thing that has a worse stench, a stench that really gets up the nostrils. That thing is a denialist politician who has been bought. We are afflicted by quite a few of these at present. The powers that be please deliver us from them and the intolerable odour they emit!

27 February 2020

Trust Your Inner Scientist

Is science incomprehensible to you? Some sort of voodoo or black magic perhaps? Then you need to connect with your inner scientist. Otherwise known as common sense.

You see the flash of lightning, and wait to hear the thunder, counting the seconds. One, two, three, four … Then you hear the crash and rumble. And, if you hadn't figured out before now why there is a delay, as many humans over the ages would certainly have done, perhaps you might be scratching your head now. Wondering.

Wondering is not a crime. It is the first stage in a process called science.

So, for those of you who dare to wonder, here is how it works. You know that light to all intents and purposes travels instantaneously.

You only need turn on a light switch to know that. But the clap of thunder is more tardy. It takes its time. You can count it down. One, two, three, four …

Perhaps you had figured all this out, i.e that the reason for the delay is light travels much faster than sound. You have figured this out on the strength of the evidence of your eyes and ears, i.e. on observations you made with your senses.

Congratulations. This is your inner scientist at work. Common sense.

Even when science seems more complex than this simple example would have it, science is still just basic common sense. The common sense you were born with. Your survival strategy. Professional scientists may use mathematical analysis, complex instruments, and collaborative checking techniques (known as peer review) to aid them in their investigations. But these are just trappings. Scientists are not trying to pull wool over your eyes. Science is not a conspiracy or an exclusive club. Behind these trappings, science is just common sense.

Conclusions in science are reached and predictions made through evidence gleaned from the five senses. This is what makes it science. If conclusions are reached or predictions made without such evidence, it is not science.

In science, evidence is king. But some people – almost never professional scientists – deny the importance of evidence, and want us to put our common sense on hold. Nowhere is this more obvious than in the field of climate science. The culprits here are mostly people with a vested interest – one way or the other – in maintaining the activities of the fossil fuel industry. Or their lackeys.

Since 1988, the evidence has been impossible to deny, unless you want to deny common sense itself. On the basis of this evidence, we – the global community – were warned loud and clear that we must phase out fossil fuels as a large-scale source of energy for our everyday activities and, simultaneously, phase in renewables. Not doing this, we were told, will lead to environmental and economic catastrophe for our way of life.

Now, more than 30 years later, having done precious little to heed the scientists' warnings, we are seeing their predictions coming to pass in our everyday lives: global heating, inundation by the sea, drought, bushfires, increased frequency of 'once-in-a-hundred-year' weather events, etc. It is too late now for phasing in or phasing out. The consequence of our tardiness is that the necessary changes in our behaviour must be much more immediate. Like now.

Why delay? Do we really want to experience the slow collapse of civilization as we know it? Or are we happy perhaps for this to happen to our progeny?

Common sense. We were born with it. It must prevail. Or *we* shall not. It has always been thus.

12 March 2020

Dark Arts

Grant (not his real name) was born, I believe, somewhere in the 1940s, or perhaps the 1950s. When I met him in the 1980s, he had just got out of prison, having served a long custodial sentence. For first degree murder.

He had become interested, as a young man, in martial arts. Given such arts were in no way fashionable in Oz at that time, I have no idea what attracted him to them. I believe, although I can't recollect with any certainty, his particular interest was in

Kendo, which originated in Japan, and which involves the use of bamboo staves as props.

Those of the day inclined to err on the side of a generosity of spirit, and to take a more or less neutral stance on contentious issues, might have described Grant as an early adopter.

These days, in the enlightened new millennium, martial arts have become, to a large extent, mainstream. To have a black belt in karate is to be highly regarded by society in general. For some young kids, it is a preferred substitute for Scouts or Guides and, given some of the baggage that comes as part and parcel of Baden-Powell's club, it is (I think) a great deal more wholesome. But back when Grant was a young man, say in the 1960s or early 1970s, such attitudes were far from commonly held.

Back then martial arts, and particularly those of Asian origin, were highly suspect, especially in the more conservative milieu. Two decades previously, or less, Australia had been threatened with military invasion by the Japanese, and Australian POWs had been subjected to horrendous (often fatal) treatment at their hands. Then, in the 1960s and 1970s, the Australian public could not avoid hearing of 'the yellow peril' and the 'falling dominoes'. Everything north of our shores was commonly assumed to be hostile. And, of course, the White Australia Policy was just getting into its stride.

The bottom line was that Asian martial arts in these times were considered subversive. They were in the category of black arts, on a par with voodoo, satanism, and witchcraft.

So, when Grant lost his temper one day while playing pool, and accidentally killed his opponent with a billiard cue, the judge, assuming Grant had acted out the Kendo playbook, took community values into account when sentencing him. He threw the book at Grant. He ruled it murder, and gave him life.

Grant did his time, excessive though it was. When he got out, he gravitated to an inner suburb of Melbourne that was then in the process of strenuously resisting gentrification, but ultimately to no avail. I lived there at the time. Presumably this made me one of the 'gentry'.

Unemployed, Grant was referred to a federally-funded training and job-placement Program of 17 weeks duration operating in his locality. The Program was designed to get people like Grant into the workforce. I worked on that Program at the time, which is how I came to know Grant. I taught workplace mathematics and computer skills.

∼

Perhaps I might digress. I think you should know a little about the Program and the part I played in it.

The Department of Social Security (DSS), as it was then known, referred clients to us. The human clay they wanted us to knead was quite a mixture. There were many Asians, some whose presence was not altogether legal, coming to grips with English as a second language. There were people with specific problems, like drug addiction, alcoholism, a criminal record, schizophrenia, bipolar disorder, physical disabilities, and/or an alleged propensity for suicide. There were young people just out of school and unable to find a job. There were people of all ages who were presently down on their luck. And there were people who had done time for murder.

… talking of suicide, we did have one actual instance over the decade or so the Program ran. The debriefing process we staff felt obliged at the time to convene for the benefit of her fellow clients (and of ourselves) was pretty intense I can tell you …

Yes indeed, the range of clients with whom we dealt was diverse to a fault. There was even one of the co-producers of an iconic Australian film with international acclaim who turned up. I knew him.

What are you doing here? I asked (as you would).

Shit happens, he replied.

In my life, I have worked in a variety of environments but this was, by the legendary country mile, the best job I have ever had. I lived only a few hundred metres from where I worked. Easy walking distance. The staff were highly skilled and adept at handling the inauspicious clientele. The work was challenging and endlessly fascinating. At the end of each 17-week intake, clients and staff would part close to tears. We had become, in this short time, a close-knit family.

I have maintained contact with one of my former clients to this day. She too was a murderer. It was her claim to fame back then, but she has others today that are more acceptable in decent society. I feel privileged to count her among my friends. She will certainly be reading this blog.

Sadly, the Program ran for just under a decade. As is prone to happen to successful programs, it was de-funded. By the then Keating government. But governments of either political stripe are wont, at a whim, to deliver a bullet to the brain when it comes to successful Programs such as ours was. Their finger is always on the trigger.

∼

Back to Grant.

Grant and I got along well. I sensed he was thoroughly institutionalized. We, the staff, had to work hard to gain his trust, because he did not take kindly to people he did not know. Although he had no trouble learning new skills or brushing up on old ones, I guessed we were going to have difficulty slotting him into conventional employment.

Some mornings on my way to walk, I would come across him walking his two Staffordshire terriers, his best friends.

One day, Grant presented at the Program in an extremely distressed state. It took us time to calm him down. Then he told us his story. Apparently, two of the local constabulary had come across him in the street where he was walking his Staffies.

We know who you are, one of them had said, and you're not fucking welcome around here.

If you don't make yourself scarce, the other had said, we'll shoot your fucking dogs.

Andy (not his real name) was Director of the Program. He got on the blower to the local cop-shop. Things were sorted out, and I can only hope, but without a great deal of confidence, that the two renegade cops were hauled over the coals.

Grant stayed in the district and continued on the Program. But I never saw him walking his Staffies in the streets again after that. His faith in humanity had received a significant setback, and we had to work on him overtime to regain his confidence. It should never have come to that.

So we approached the 13-week mark of the 17-week Program. It was time for clients to ready themselves for their trial work placements. Andy was a whizz at organizing these, and he found one for Grant despite the latter's unfortunate background. The CEO of a small private company with quarters in the CBD, was prepared to give people like Grant a second chance. He offered Grant a clerical role in his organization.

Come Monday morning of week 13, and our premises were empty of clients. They were all out on their trial placements. The staff were on deck, engaged in preparation for the next intake, and in other sundry desk duties. The premises were uncharacteristically quiet. It was in the nature of our client group, when present, to be vocal and demonstrative. There was always somebody's prize ox being gored. Personal dysfunction quickly became communal dysfunction in this milieu. We constantly had bombs to defuse. So we cherished peace when it came.

Peace was not to last. At lunch time, Grant was back, verging on the hysterical. We calmed him down and tried to coax the story out of him. Though he was incoherent and effectively unable to communicate in any useful sense, we managed slowly to piece things together. Apparently, he found the office environment unbearably hostile. Given he was not inclined to trust people until they proved themselves worthy of it, perhaps this should not have come as a surprise to us. He was a claustrophobe. An agoraphobe. A social isolate. His time in the slammer had not prepared him for anything like the interactions with people that came with a conventional office job.

So, we asked ourselves, where to from here? Do we give up on Grant? We had skilled him up heroically, but placing him in employment looked like an impossibly hard ask. Unfortunately, job placement was the main brief with which we had been entrusted by DSS and, ultimately, by the government of the day who were funding us. Should we concede failure in Grant's case?

This story has a happy ending. Fate solved the problem for us. What happened to Grant was an unlikely story, in the nature of an urban legend, that most of us have heard but think only happens in la la land. But I vouch it *did* happen to Grant.

At just the right moment, an uncle, well set up but with no direct descendants, died. In his will, he left Grant his farm with ancillaries in Central Victoria. Grant retired there and, assuming he is still alive, would almost certainly be there to this day. I imagine him, a virtual recluse, picking up the necessary farming skills, and successfully putting them into practice. He was not a slow learner. And I imagine there might be a couple of farm dogs running round the traps, much loved by their owner.

The tooth fairy is alive and well. Fairy tales do happen. Just ask Grant. If you can get him to trust you.

COVID and Associated Privations

26 March 2020

Going Viral

Yes, the inevitable silliness has happened. I know of people who will not drink Corona beer because they believe it carries the dreaded virus.

It would do no good to call the 'coronavirus' by its more specific abbreviated form of COVID-19. Or, as my veterinarian daughter would pedantically insist, SARS-2-CoV. Because these acronyms sound like imprecations against cockroaches, it's likely the supermarket shelves would be emptied of insect baits overnight.

Which brings me to the problematic issue people don't seem to be able to get out of their pea-brains: toilet paper. Too much has been made of this issue already. Can I just add tangentially that if the problem were an outbreak of gastro-enteritis rather than of a coronavirus, a consistent but perverse reaction might be a rush on hair conditioner.

And of course we all know those armadillo-eating Asians were the cause of it all. We were right to impose entry restrictions on these yellow people. Otherwise they might come here and start eating our koalas. If they can find any after the bushfires.

Do you think, given the power of shock-jocks and social media, we can ever hope that rational discourse at times of crisis will prevail?

In the meantime, please don't let Donald Trump know about Corona, the beer that is. Otherwise we can expect him to start rattling on about those raping and murdering Mexicans waging biological warfare from across the border.

Joking aside. This is serious.

The lesson we can learn, if we have not already learnt it, is to block our ears when the megaphone mouths are sounding off. Misinformation is never a good look but, in present circumstances with a potentially lethal virus doing the rounds, it could have lethal consequences. Never was it more important to give the big A to those inimical shock-jocks, to the social media cowboys, and to the neighbour next-door who likes the sound of his own voice.

Treat these people as your worst enemies. Because that's what they are.

The voices we should be listening to are invariably quiet. Their message is evidence based and hence informed. Seek them out. Your life could depend on it.

Don't horde stuff. It does no good and may do harm.

Wash your hands.

Keep others at a safe distance.

Etc., etc. You know he drill. You've heard it often enough. Do it.

Oh, and seek your stiff upper lip. Look for some form of catharsis. This may be done through (1) horror or (2) humour.

For horror appropriate to the occasion, try reading the Edgar Allan Poe short story, *The Masque of the Red Death*. It should freak you out big time.

For humour, I cannot think of a better example than the story I tell below. This, I swear, is an event that really happened. It just goes to show that children of any age can teach us adults a thing or two, even in the most trying of times.

A friend of mine, whom I shall call Sandra, is the mother of a nine-year-old girl, whom I shall call Vida. Sandra and Vida went to the local IGA supermarket. As soon as she was inside, young Vida, on a mission, tore away from her mother and went hurtling down one of the aisles. She came back loaded with multiple twelve-packs of toilet paper. So many, in fact, you could hardly see the tiny head of the little person somewhere beneath.

Look mummy, said Vida. I'm panic-buying.

I swear that kid has a rosy future in stand-up comedy.

23 April 2020

Aloneness

Please excuse me should you find this post/blog to be a rambling affair. All over the shop like a dog's breakfast, as they say. Like life itself.

I know I am privileged. I have retired from paid work, and I have the wherewithal to support myself. So I write novels. By its nature, this is a solitary activity. But I don't mind this at all. And it didn't take me any time at all to get accustomed to it when it became mandatory. It's not so very different from the way I've been living all along.

So 'lock-down' owing to Covid hardly feels foreign to me. I have a loving partner. The Coles supermarket delivers to my door.

My coastal environment is extremely pleasant, and right there on my doorstep. I have plenty to do. I use Zoom when I want to talk to grandkids. My exercise regime is a 3-kilometre walk on the beach. In a typical day, I might see half a dozen people in the flesh. At an appropriate social distance.

I am loath to crow about this too much. I recognize most other people are doing it much tougher than I am. My children, for example, all of whom live in big cities, are gearing themselves up to work potentially from home, while – one of them at least together with spouse – has to manage kids who are *learning* at home. At the *same* home, for pity's sake!

There are people who are dedicated extroverts, for whom the company of others is like the oxygen they breathe. They, I imagine, are beyond stir crazy.

There are those trapped at home in an abusive relationship. Wtf are *they* meant to do?

And let's not forget those in their late teens, early twenties, and beyond, whose chance of a physical relationship with a beloved partner is necessarily put on ice. How are these people, post-Covid, expected to engage in – quaint word, I know – courtship?

So, when I talk about my privileged situation, can I perhaps expect these people to show me the finger? Or can I anticipate, contrariwise, that my example might point them in the direction of paths of their own making that might help guide them through the crisis?

Very important to me, I embrace and am embraced by visual and aural arts of my choice. All the time. Let me deal in this blog with the visual.

I enjoy *ukiyo-e* every day. They hang on my walls and draw my eye constantly. They are dear to me, almost like friends. For the benefit of the uninitiated, *ukiyo-e* are Japanese woodblock prints. The anonymous beauty depicted in the picture above is an example. It is the work of Susuki Harunobu. He trod this earth from 1724 to 1770.

If you have read my earlier blog/posts, you will realize I love things Japanese. When, one way or another, the present pandemic comes to an end, I shall visit Japan again. The Japanese, so I would argue, do not deal so much in 'sights' (think the Eiffel Tower or the Grand Canyon) as with 'events'. Taking in a 'sight' is a passive and detached activity. Only the sight gets to have an input. You do not.

By contrast, experiencing an 'event' is very much an interactive activity. An event is something you are part of. It makes its mark on you, and you on it.

The Japanese are masters at turning 'sights' into 'events'. Even a visit to a shopping mall or a train station can become an event in Japan. At the Sendai Railway Station on my last visit to Japan, I found the entire Sendai Philharmonic Orchestra there playing Beethoven. The audience of commuters, frozen in their tracks at first, were soon literally hopping to the beat. So was I. Can you imagine this happening in Grand Central Station? Or *Gare du Nord*? Or Southern Cross Station?

To move around Japan is to experience one event after another, most of them unexpected. Life becomes exciting.

And, of course, you don't just drink tea in Japan. You participate in a tea ceremony.

My woodblock print (above) seems to reflect this. When I look at the lady in it (as I do daily), she seems to be inviting me to share one of her most private moments with her. And the landscapes and seascapes of Utagawa Hiroshige (1797-1858) seem to invite me not merely to look at them but to come on in. I cannot resist.

What do you do if *ukiyo-e* is not your bag? Well, visuals with the ability to engage are not the sole privilege of humans to create. Nature does a pretty good job. At present, when I go out onto my front verandah, I see the air filled with blue-grey butterflies, all – for reasons best know to themselves – heading north.

The air is so thick with them I imagine that, should I chance to yawn, I might swallow half a dozen or more of them. It is a beautiful 'sight' to behold and, if I really did swallow some of them, it would be an 'event' to experience.

11 June 2020

Spectacles and Screaming Horrors

I took this photo in Japan in 2019, when international travel was still a possibility. It was springtime in the northern hemisphere. This is the iconic and much-photographed Megane-bashi, or Spectacles Bridge, in central Nagasaki. It gets its nickname, of course, because of its likeness to a pair of spectacles when considered together with its reflection in the water. My intended focus when I took this snap, was the lovely bridge itself, gracing as it does the old town. But inadvertently, I caught a moment of fun among the young girls enjoying the fine weather and the glorious surrounds.

Inadvertency in photography is, by definition, unpredictable, but can be a priceless pearl when it does happen.

Spectacles and Screaming Horrors | 89

… it can also be a visceral shock to the system. I am reminded of a (possibly apocryphal) story I heard about a couple driving round Europe. They came across a car that had gone off the road and presumably left abandoned in a ditch. They stopped to photograph it. When, much later, they examined the detail of the photos in the comfort of their hotel, they discovered there were two dead bodies in the car …

Now examine the detail of my photo. Look closely at the folk in it. I promise you won't find anything near so ghoulish as is to be found in the above anecdote. Just loads of charm, such as often comes my way when I travel round Japan.

What is the schoolgirl in the blue skirt at front right photographing? Further up the waterway is a group of four girls out of uniform, three of which have curled the fingers of their fists round their eyes to mimic spectacles.

And the other uniformed schoolgirl balancing on one of the stepping stones gives me a feeling of vertigo, and gets me hoping she won't fall. I want to reach out and save her. I needn't have worried. There was no way in the world she was going to fall.

Now you may be wondering why I have posted a blog that on the surface is such a total non-event. Well, I don't believe it is good for our health to regard such things as non-events.

A lot depends on the mental perspective of the person – you – taking it in. Especially in trying times like these, I believe a lot is to be gained by focusing on simple pleasures where possible. Taking delight in events of such innocence can enable us to better see the context of things of greater moment. Especially when we are overwhelmed on a daily basis by grim news of 'moment'. I call them screaming horrors. Happy people, perhaps young like these, have much to bring to our lives if we will give them the chance.

We have a tendency to focus too much on the screaming horrors of our day. The media, mainstream and otherwise, are complicit in this. Look at the current scene in the USA. The media tell us – and of course we reserve the right to believe them or not – that the place is packed full of screaming horrors of many stripes. Medical and economic emergencies. Entrenched racial intolerance. Unprecedented civil unrest. Where will it end?

And, while on the subject of screaming horrors, let's not forget that one such – the daddy of all screaming horrors – an armed nuclear weapon – was exploded over northern Nagasaki – the beautiful city of my photograph – city of innocent schoolchildren who didn't ask for or expect such a horror – on 9 August 1945.

We should stay aware of the screaming horrors. Knowledge of a problem is the first step in dealing effectively with it. And attempting to deal with such problems – such cancers on the body of our common humanity – as they arise is, I believe, our humanitarian duty.

But be aware also of our collective need for therapy. And what could be more therapeutic for us all than occasionally tuning into the voices of happy children like those in my photo?

25 June 2020

Choices

Once in a while, there is a diabolic symmetry in the choices we have to make. *Sophie's Choice* is a novel by William Styron, adapted for film in the 1980s. Sophie Zawistowska, played by Meryl Streep, faced one such symmetry: which of her two children to sacrifice to Nazi brutality. I know the basics of the story (most of us do), but I have never actually seen the film. I don't think I ever shall. I doubt I could bear to.

Now we see the diabolic symmetry again. Those around the world, including in Australia, who feel they ought to protest in the cause of Black Lives Matter, are faced with it. Do they choose to protest and thereby, in all likelihood, contribute to the spread of Covid-19, and to deaths from such? Or do they choose *not* to protest and thereby, in all likelihood, contribute through complacency to the epidemic of black deaths?

Let's look at each choice in turn. Most people would agree Black Lives Matter is a worthy cause. But Covid-19 does not respect causes humans deem worthy. It respects causes viruses deem worthy. Its mission is to colonize human body cells, using them as factories to churn out clones at exponential rates, destroying the colonized cell, and sometimes the host body, in the process. A mass protest of humans provides it with the ideal conditions in which to fulfill its mission. Ergo: we should not protest.

Now let's look at the other choice. Black deaths in custody have persisted over the years with very little done by governments except token acknowledgement of the problem. This tokenism extended to an ineffectual Royal Commission charged to the Australian taxpayer and whose recommendations were mostly left unaddressed. Protest appears to be the only avenue remaining. Black deaths caused by custody and by other attempts to enforce law, exceed those resulting from Covid-19. Ergo: we should protest.

So here is the diabolic symmetry mirroring that with which Sophie was faced.

It is not helpful to dub those who choose to join protests as 'selfish'. Would it have helped Sophie? It is the nature of such choices that, if one option can be regarded as 'selfish', the other must necessarily be regarded as 'selfless'. Therein lies the diabolic symmetry, the other side of the same coin.

What was *my* choice? Well, there were no protests running in Rockhampton, my nearest population centre. Perhaps I should have been a lone protester like Greta Thunberg. But no. I didn't protest. I can only applaud those in capital cities who did. They were faced with a diabolical choice. And they were brave enough to make it.

9 July 2020

Aspects of Narcisism

Narcissism involves a very limited view of life. And often that's the very reason narcissists hold narcissism to their bosoms. They like limits. Life with limits feels safe. Life without limits feels frightening.

It is said that the current President of the United States is a narcissist. Could that make him a very limited and frightened man? Limited and limit*ing*. Frightened and frighten*ing*.

Narcissism has some close cousins with names like self-love, self-absorption, solipsism, etc. For those heading for the dictionary, let me tell you what Wikipedia says about solipsism. Solipsism is the philosophical notion that only one's own mind is sure to exist. That lets Donald Trump off the hook. The man has never had a philosophical notion in his life. Nor much of a mind, some would argue.

Speaking of minds, there's a concept perhaps related to narcissism that psychologists call 'theory of mind'. Wikipedia has a succinct definition of this also. Theory of mind is the ability to attribute mental states to oneself and to others. All going well, we develop theory of mind at the age of four or five. *Before that*, we are all little narcissists. *After that*, we are aware other people have minds just like we do, and that the notions in their minds may be different from those in our minds.

… what an extraordinary idea! At age three or thereabouts, it would appear we regard everything external to us as 'mindless'. All those people feeding us, caring for us, doting on us, teaching us the rudiments of language, are nothing more than robotic attendants on us. We alone are blessed with a mind …

Psychologists have developed ingenious tests for the presence (or absence) of theory of mind. You can look them up on Wikipedia. They, the psychologists, have concluded that humans, other primates, and certain non-primate animals exhibit theory of mind. Nobody who has been around domestic dogs could doubt that dogs have theory of mind. But as for domestic cats, well, some people might have doubts about them. Is this being uncharitable to moggies?

People on the autism spectrum are often considered to have an underdeveloped theory of mind. So they are lacking to some degree in social skills, and are fearful of moving outside their comfort zone. This does *not* mean they are less intelligent. Nor does it mean they are mentally deranged. Some people 'on the spectrum' have prodigious skills in a particular area, e.g. in memory, or in *sitzfleisch* (or stick-at-it-ness). We should learn to understand, and then to tolerate, their deficiencies. And we should respect, and then stand in awe of, their special skills. To wit, Greta Thunberg perhaps.

Back to my musings on narcissism. I'd like to coin the phrase 'mutual narcissism'. I'm not inventing anything new. In fact, there's a word there for it already. 'Tribalism'. To each person in a tribe, his/her fellow members are just his/her reflection returned. Tribalism then, like narcissism, is often motivated by fear and a yearning for limits. Right now, in 2020, there is plenty around to be be concerned about. And plenty to incite a craving for limits. Bushfires, Covid, lockdown, climate change, China, unemployment, ... The list just goes on and on.

So, rather than deal with these big issues head-on, applying logic and science as necessary, we have an urge to take the easy way out, i.e. retreat to our chosen tribe, wherein we feel safe.

Some tribes are benign, e.g. affiliation to a football team. By way of family heritage I, for example, am nominally a Carlton supporter – we're talking AFL here – although my support over the years has been lukewarm to say the least. More loyal supporters (one-eyed, it could be said) see everything through the prism of their team affiliation. A Carlton supporter, for example, would never ever see eye-to-eye with a Collingwood supporter. It's a brand of mutual narcissism that comes with the territory.

Other tribes are not so benign. Some are dangerously counterproductive. Rusted-on affiliation to a political party. Political populism. Zealous Christianity to the exclusion of alternatives, especially (for the times in which we live) Muslims. Ditto for zealous Islam. Racism and all other notions of ethnic superiority. Anti-vaxism. Flat-earthism. Active distrust of science. Adherence to any one of a number of crackpot conspiracy theories doing the rounds. The list knows no end. If you are in want of a malign tribe to which to belong, don't look any further than the manipulators on social media, or on *Sky News* after dark, or on shock-jock radio. There's something there for everyone. With each and every one a poisoned chalice.

Tribalism. It all starts with fear of what we don't know, or don't understand, or feel overwhelmed by. Never was a truer word spoken, nor one more crucial for our times, than: 'the only thing we have to fear is fear itself'.

23 July 2020

First Contact

A ntarctica. In 2006. Allow me to reminisce.
This gorgeous leopard seal was probably making his/her first ever contact with humans when I snapped her/him. Doesn't he/she look as surprised as all get-out? Like she/he is thinking: 'Am I dreaming?' Or perhaps 'Could this be a nightmare?'

There would, I'd hazard a guess, be no Covid-19 in Antarctica at present. Nevertheless, we can't go there. The truth is there are not too many places we *can* go. Not right now. We can only entertain delicious fantasies by drooling over photos like this. You would certainly have some photos too, though not necessarily of Antarctica, over which to drool.

So, as I have already asked of you, let me indulge in fond reminiscence.

We travelled south from Hobart on a Russian vessel described as 'ice-strengthened', i.e. able to push through thin pancake ice, but not equipped to break the heavy stuff. She (boats are feminine naturally) was named Marina Tsvetaeva, after the revered Russian poet. It was February, the end of summer in the southern hemisphere. There were about sixty people plus crew on the boat. Quite intimate. From Hobart, it was four days rough sailing before we reached the coast of the Antarctic continent. Near Shackleton's hut. Near the Ross Ice Shelf. South of the Antarctic Circle.

What can I say about Antarctica that hasn't already been said? It should hardly surprise you that I found it quite unlike any other place I had ever been. The colours needed to be seen to be believed. Unreal shades of pink, orange, and red (sun very low in the sky), of blue (icebergs), and of course white in thirty different shades. A feeling of isolation not realizable anywhere else in the world. Glaciers, one of my very favourite natural phenomena, slithering and grinding at glacial speed, dominating the foreground and reaching to distant horizons.

So what were the circumstances in play when (may I dare to presume?) the leopard seal made first contact with this small contingent of humans of which I was part, or indeed with humanity at large? When he/she first became aware such things as humans even existed? It was about three in the morning Eastern Australian Time. But the time didn't really have much meaning in this place where the sun barely ever sets in summer and barely ever rises in winter. So it was bright daylight. About six or seven of us were exploring the northern reaches of the Ross Ice Shelf in a Zodiac, which is an inflatable rubber dinghy.

The temperature was about minus three degrees Celcius. We had been taking in the sights now for almost two straight hours so, even though we were rugged up for the occasion in our very warmest gear, the penetrating cold was beginning to bite. We had resorted to tapping our feet on the floor of the Zodiac to keep warm. We were hanging out for breakfast back at the Marina Tsvetaeva, especially for the cup of hot chocolate that would accompany it.

Then we rounded the corner of an ice wall, and came across that wondrous sight in the photo. Our eyeball to eyeball moment. Of an astonished leopard seal, seeing humans for the first time. Relaxing after a hearty breakfast of penguin sashimi. Toto, this is not Kansas anymore.

Let's review the animal kingdom apropos the response of its individual members to humans. I warrant every kangaroo in Australia knows a human when he/she sees one. Lions in the Kruger National Park would, I suspect, be very blase about if not totally bored by people. Cows in India roam freely among the human population as if they were their brothers/sisters.

But this Antarctic animal was, I suspect, in a different category entirely.

There was no terror in the creature's face. No fear of the unknown. Just a kind of astonishment. This was his/her territory, and she/he was sovereign here. His/her surroundings were familiar and safe. We, the strange ones, were the strangers here, the fish out of water, so how could we possibly be any sort of threat?

We gawked, took photos, and bedded down memories. Then, in our Zodiac, we moved on. The moment of magic had come and gone. The leopard seal went back to letting regular leopard seal thoughts flood its leopard seal brain. We went back to letting thoughts of a warm breakfast flood ours.

First contact was over. Will there be another?

27 Aug 2020

WAFER

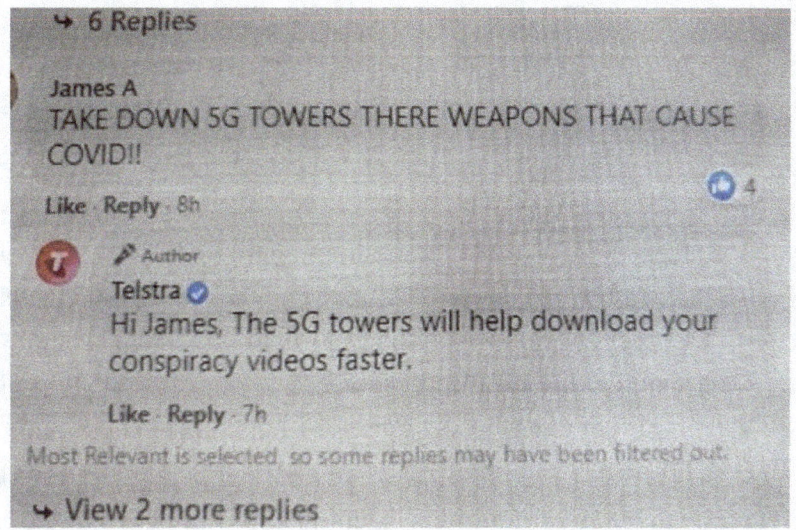

He said: I'm worried about this 5G technology. It sounds very dangerous.
She said: What do you propose to do about it?
He said: I think I'll do some research on Facebook.
She said: OMG.

Research on Facebook? Doesn't he know 'research' and 'Facebook' don't go together in the same sentence? *Anybody* can post *anything* on Facebook and, given the number of certifiable nutjobs out there ready and eager to do just this, the site is *not* the place to go when you plan to pursue a line of inquiry.

Save Facebook for your family photos, cheery messages, and 'likes'. That's what it does best.

So where might one go in order to research 5G? Well, I know

it doesn't sound at all sexy, but why not start with a high-school physics textbook? In the index at the back, you should find 'electromagnetic radiation'. That's ten syllables, so let's shorten it to EMR.

Shock horror! The dreaded R-word. Radiation. Isn't that the stuff of nuclear bombs, and out-of-control nuclear reactors? An invisible killer. Think Hiroshima, Chernobyl, Fukushima.

Sorry to disabuse you. EMR has been on this earth before we humans were. We live in a soup of EMR. We evolved to live in harmony with it and, as a result, we cannot survive without it. Fortunately, the laws of physics have it that all objects, living and non-living, with a temperature above absolute zero (roughly -273 C), emit oodles and oodles of EMR. You, sitting in your +20 C living room, are a powerhouse of EMR production.

Most EMR in nature is benign. Our earth has an ozone layer protecting us from most of the dangerous stuff coming from space, the high frequency end of the EMR spectrum and lots more besides. In fact, because this benign EMR is everywhere around us, it really should be regarded as a fifth element after the quartet of Earth Air Fire and Water that was once recognized throughout the ancient world. Earth Air Fire Water and Radiation. I suggest we use the acronym WAFER to represent these five things on which our life is so dependent. We all love acronyms, don't we?

So where does 5G fit into all this?

Radio, TV, wi-fi, and all the Gs from two to five, make use of an extremely benign portion of the spectrum – to which we have given the name 'radio waves' – of the already quite benign soup through which we swim. Early in the 20th century, people began to realize they could exploit these radio waves. Through a process known as modulation, they found they could send signals with the wave as carrier. Modulating the waves does not make them suddenly more dangerous than the regular radio waves found in nature.

Think of carrier pigeons. Through the processes of breeding and training, we can get pigeons to carry messages taped to their legs. But carrier pigeons are no more dangerous than regular pigeons that haven't been bred or trained. They are not about to peck our eyes out.

And, for crying out loud, that's all 5G is. No, not trained pigeons, but radio waves carrying messages for us. These waves are not about to fry our brains. They are not the cause of Covid-19. They are stuff humans have lived with for millennia, during which Da Vinci, Shakespeare, Beethoven, Newton, and Einstein thrived. And you and I.

So, before you take up with nutjobs and embrace their conspiracy theories, consider this in summary:

WAFER has been around for miillions if not billions of years. That includes the R for Radiation. Because we evolved on a planet drenched in WAFER, we cannot do without it. Without WAFER we would not exist. And 5G, just like 2G 3G and 4G before it, is nothing more than an extremely benign form of R for Radiation whose use to transmit messages we, clever mob that we are, have learnt to harness. Let's not burn down 5G towers. Instead let's enjoy the benefits they have to offer.

He said: I'm so glad you've clarified that for me.

She said: Don't mention it.

He said: But I'm very worried about vaccinations. I saw on Facebook they cause autism.

She said: OMG.

8 October 2020

Road Trip in the Country of Queensland

OMG. The *country* of Queensland? Shall we be issuing passports next? And shall the likely lad in the photo be our first prime minister/president? We found him near Jericho, a wide place in the road in Central Queensland. The locals there like to decorate their termite mounds in such fashion. Bush arts are alive and well in this neck of the woods, and here is proof.

We had been planning a trip to Japan for October, but the world has changed. I can't even travel to the other States. States? Or Territories? At least that's what they were formerly known as. You know: New South Wales, Victoria, etc. The seven points on the large star adorning the flag of the country formerly known as 'Australia'. The man elected Prime Minister of this erstwhile country, some seventeen short months ago, now keeps running around trying to pretend he's still in charge.

You think my language is hyperbolic? Give me a break. I'm just putting into words the way things feel like to me.

So, with borders effectively closed, owing to Covid, in all directions, my partner (Janet) and I set off on a road trip within our brand-new country. I mean the Country of Queensland. It's been many a long year since we ventured on a road trip. It's now not only a presenting possibility, but a present necessity. If we want to travel at all, that is.

My younger daughter, Cathy, has fewer possibilities for travel. She lives in a country (formerly a State) of Covid lepers known as Victoria. This is a small country, like Belgium is within Europe, so she has much less room to move than have Janet and I. Moreover, last time I spoke to her, viz. to my daughter, her lockdown conditions forbade her to move more than 5 kilometres from home. She lives in this home with husband and four young children. All six inhabitants of this home are working or studying from home.

Are they stir crazy? Do dogs have fleas?

So I promised I would text her one photo every day whilst on my road trip. That was the *least* I could do.

Trouble is, my phone is with Optus. Some of the remote places we go to (like Winton which is where we were just a few days back) are not covered by Optus. I think I may have to post the daily photos on Facebook, but this seems much less personal. Which is a pity, because my daughter had been so looking forward to living vicariously via my daily texted photos. No good telling her to get a life. What other options are available to her?

I feel very sorry for Cathy, and for the predicament in which she finds herself. But what more can I do? A microscopic virus is dictating the terms here.

What, then, have I discovered on our road trip round our brand new country? Well, the dinosaur sites at and near Winton and Richmond have the capacity to astound all who venture there bar the totally brain-dead. Who would not be moved by the visual evidence of a dinosaur stampede, involving three different species of dinosaur, at Lark's Quarry outside of Winton? My message to all citizens of Queensland is: get out there and see it. There is nothing like this anywhere else in the world.

We'll be back.

Another remarkable phenomenon we encountered out there in regional Queensland was the sheer volume of traffic. People who would normally be holidaying in Bali, Fiji, and the like, were hitting the road in outback Queensland. Businesses – hotels, restaurants, tour outfits, and so forth – that imagined they were cactus just two months ago, were now finding themselves snowed under. It's a brave traveller out there who fails to book things in advance. Don't expect to just rock up any more. That may have worked prior to 2020. Different rules now apply.

So 2020 has been a year of total surprises. But not all of them have been unpleasant. Our road trip has been a wonder. If you'll permit me a cliche, often used these days, one should never waste a good crisis.

5 November 2020

Accordion to Trump

Recognize this guy? Is he familiar? I'll give you a clue. He has a habit of waving his tiny hands back and forth horizontally while he spews his trademark bile from his tiny mouth. So some clever person decided to mock up a video in which an accordion (FAKE NEWS!) is inserted between his paws. Look it up for yourself on YouTube. It's hilarious, but also a tad frightening.

Here in Australia, we can't believe the shenanigans we see coming out of the USA on a daily basis. Appalled, most of us laugh and hope/pray for the sake of the world the aberration will pass. Some of us, like my partner Janet, born in Oakland California, worry themselves sick, and can't drag themselves away from CNN, FOX, Al Jazzera, RT, NHK, and any other foreign channel offering commentary on the issue. It is an addiction for her as profound as any chemical substance.

Every now and again, she stirs from her addiction-induced coma on the couch, and mutters (pathetically) something like, 'He's going to win, he's going to win,' while chewing her fingernails down to the elbows. I, born in Sydney Australia, have to reassure her that not all the 60% plus of the 150 million plus registered voters in the USA that actually cast a vote are going to be fooled by this dangerous clown. Surely there is some intelligent life on the other side of the Pacific.

3rd November 2020 can't come soon enough for me, so I can have my Janet back. Of course, there's no certainty/likelihood the circus will end on Nov 3. Why should the circus stop just because the accordionist has been told to quit the stage? There's more than a chance his unwelcome performance will continue until Inauguration Day in January 2021, or even beyond.

One day, it will all stop. Nothing's surer. And then, hallelujah, Janet shall have to go cold turkey.

2 December 2020

The City of Iquique, the Nitrate Bubble, and What We Can All Learn from It

Iquique (pronounced ikeeka) is a city in northern Chile you probably haven't heard of. Janet and I were there in October 2016. I'm so glad we paid the city a visit, because it's one of the more fascinating places I've visited in that country or, for that matter, anywhere in the wide world. We didn't spend near enough time there in 2016, so I feel compelled to pay it a second visit, this time allowing a lot more time to explore. It's on my 'must do' list once Covid is behind us. I'm not holding my breath.

Iquique is unlike any other place I have ever visited. On the fringes of the Atacama desert, its average number of rainy days per year is less than one. One promotional website I visited gives it a year-round daily maximum temperature of around 24 C. That really does sound too good to be true, but I vouch that life was very very bearable during my brief visit. If surfing or paragliding is your bag, and you have independent means, you might consider learning Spanish and emigrating.

To the immediate west of Iquique is the Pacific Ocean and, since earthquakes are *de rigueur* hereabouts, the city is under constant threat of tsunamis from this direction, as many warning signs around the city streets will tell you. To the immediate east of Iquique, and rising to heights of around 800 metres, is the *cordillera de la costa*, including a range of dunes to take the breath away, and which seemingly threatens to bury the city in a tsunami of sand at any moment. It is from the dizzying heights of these dunes that paragliders can indulge their adrenalin-charged passion.

Still further east is the full-on Atacama desert and, beyond that, the incredible Andean *cordillera*, rising to heights of between 4,000 metres and 7,000 metres. You may brave such heights as long as you feel no compulsion to breathe air.

If all that seems daunting, you can relax at a few metres only above sea level in the central square, *Plaza Prat*, in Iquique. Here you will be entertained by the street culture, comprising some of the best buskers I have seen anywhere in the world. Melbourne and Sydney eat your hearts out. You are not in the same league.

Another thing you can do in *Plaza Prat*, or just about anywhere in Chile for that matter, is sip on a pisco sour or three, a drink to which I quickly became quite partial.

Re street culture and buskers: see the photo above for an

example. Re pisco sour: it is more for the taste buds and the neuroreceptors of the brain than for the eye.

Now, while you are looking at this photo, please do not fail to notice to notice the building in the background, whose facade contains Moorish arches in blue and white, and a heavily carved solid wooden door. It is *Casino Espanol*, a rich gentleman's club from Iquique's heyday, and now by all reports a classy restaurant. The club was for nitrate barons, from the days of the boom late in the 19th and early in the 20th century. Back then, the economy of Iquique, and that of Chile as a whole, was heavily reliant on the mining of nitrate in the form of saltpetre. Most of the world back then bought nitrate from Chile to make munitions and/or fertilizer. War and/or agriculture. Just the ticket. The world was addicted of course. Chile had a virtual monopoly on this versatile commodity, and Iquique, happily, was at the epicentre of it all.

We were interested to see the interior of *Casino Espanol*, having heard from guidebooks that it was well worth a look. But, drat, that wooden door was locked. We sat down nearby with coffee and cake while we plotted our next move. While we were so engaged, a chubby fellow came along with a key and unlocked the door. Janet was by his side in a flash, to ask him if he would let us inside. Not only did he allow us in, but he opted for the next hour or so to be our personal guide.

Inside, was a cave that would upstage Aladdin's. Dim lighting, steel scaffolding bolted together, stepladders scraping the ceilings, plaster dust on the carpeted floors, etc., all added to the effect, and told of renovations in progress. The last vestiges of a gentleman's club were being erased to make way for the trappings of a high class restaurant. Out with the old, in with the new. Our guide, it turned out, was in charge of these renovations and – presumably under orders – was not inclined to compromise. I hesitate to think what treasures were about to be lost in the process. I suspect the enchanting nooks and crannies would be largely done away with, in favour of an open plan, more accommodating to tables in a high-class restaurant.

Aladdin's cave? Treasures? Everywhere there seemed to be nooks and crannies leading off to other nooks and crannies, all separated by gorgeous Moorish arches, and containing paintings, frescoes, mosaics, and sculptures of considerable beauty, all harking from the *fin de siecle*. Don Quixote was a repeating theme of many of these art works. A grand staircase led up to another level where the beauty repeated itself. Everywhere there was candy for the eye. Everywhere was overwhelming.

I lined up my camera for a shot into the interior of one of the crannies, only to find in my view somebody intending to photograph *me*. Who was this gringo? Wasn't this a private tour? Then I realized I was looking at my own reflection. Full-length mirrors were strewn throughout the precincts like booby traps throughout a battle zone. These mirrors multiplied the space. As a consequence, this enchanted cave appeared to have oodles more nooks and crannies than, in fact, it actually did.

Many of the crannies sported small bookshelves whose contents would have once served the refined tastes of nitrate barons and their entourage. Now I guessed these dusty volumes were destined for landfill. Our guide invited us to help ourselves to anything on these shelves that took our fancy. Feeling we were being urged to participate in a form of cultural vandalism, we hesitated there for a bit. But, in the end, we half-reluctantly chose one. Most were in Spanish, of course, but one was in English. It was an 1887 translation from the Latin of the collected works of Horace. Now who the freak reads Horace these days? Apparently, though, for the elite of Iquique in the late 19th century, Horace was hot stuff.

We took it.

Having been dazzled by magic for an hour or so, we thanked our de facto guide, leaving the truly remarkable *Casino Espanol* with great reluctance. But, *voila*, there were plenty of other relics of bygone days to be found in the city of Iquique. Lining picturesque *Calle Baquedano*, there were period mansions for the nitrate barons, out of colourful timber, in a style we had never ever seen before. And there was the beautiful former opera house, also under restoration, which, in the 1890s had been 'on the circuit' and had hosted divas from all over the world.

But it not my primary intention in this blog to provide a travelogue for this remarkable city. I'll leave that to *Lonely Planet* and the like. The brief I have chosen is to look at the way the nitrate bubble burst early in the 20th century, and to see what lessons this might have for those of us inhabiting the 21st. So how did the bubble burst?

During WWI in Germany, a chemist by the name of Fritz Haber found a way to synthesize ammonia from its constituent elements, nitrogen and hydrogen, winning a Nobel Prize for his troubles. After such synthesis, it was a simple step to oxidize the ammonia to produce nitrate. To do this on an industrial scale turned out to be cheaper than mining nitrate. Overnight, the mainstay of the Chilean economy collapsed comprehensively. Iquique went into swift decline. Mining centres like Humberstone, just beyond the *cordillera de la costa*, became eerie ghost towns. An era ended brutally. It was all over Red Rover for nitrate mining, and almost for Chile.

Why did the bubble burst? Because of new technology.

So what lessons can we, in 21st century Australia, take from this? We, too, in this country, rely on the mining of commodities that are fast becoming redundant. Such activity is in the process of being superseded by technology that is newer, cheaper, and cleaner. It is not nitrate mining. It is fossil fuel mining. The new technology is not synthetic ammonia. It is the harvesting of renewable energy, mainly solar and wind.

To be sceptical on this point is to ignore the facts on the ground. State governments, of both political stripe, are embracing solar and wind technology. So too is big business. Why? Simple economics.

Our federal government, on the other hand, is having to be dragged kicking and screaming into the future. Why?

Chile didn't manage to dodge the bullet in the 20th century, and it paid the price. Can we dodge it in the 21st?

31 Dec 2020

Cancel 2020

If this is your inclination, I can sympathize.
The year 2020 was a beast of a year, one most of us would prefer to forget. The summer bushfires, principally the consequence of human-induced climate change, were, by any measure you care to name, the worst ever seen in Australia. B'Jesus, we thought that was bad enough. Then Covid came along.

Like the bushfires, Covid is, according to informed evidence, the unintended consequence of human disregard for the environment. Covid dictated its grizzly terms for the bulk of the year 2020. And it's not over yet. Covid was and still is the dooziest of doozies. It intends to stay the course well into 2021. Humans are such obliging hosts.

We all agree on one thing. We've had enough. We need a break for Pete's sake.

Hold it right there, won't you? Who the hell is this Pete? Perhaps we can pin the blame on him. We need a scapegoat. That way we can avoid shouldering any responsibility ourselves.

There's the rub. If we are not careful, the legacy of Covid will be worse than Covid itself. In general, people in isolation have minds like empty vessels, susceptible to being filled by any crackpot conspiracy theory, blame game, or xenophobic notion doing the rounds out there. If face-to-face human interaction won't fill minds, the nutters in cyberspace will. And they are very, very active. They sense easy pickings.

So it is we've been encouraged to believe 'greenies are arsonists', '5G causes Covid', and 'science is crap'. We are constantly warned of 'China virus', 'Kung Flu', and 'deep state'. And there are memes circulating that are even more outrageous than the above, memes verging on the deranged.

Have you heard, for example, that 'Satanic blood-drinking Hollywood elites', are behind Y, where Y is your catastrophe of choice? You mean you haven't heard? Then, dude, it's high time you did some research on the internet. It's so so easy. Disengage your brain. Suspend your capacity to discern. Get yourself on line. Believe whatever you see there. Don't ask questions. Don't you know the internet never lies?

Let's stop the sick jokes. There are certifiable nutjobs in the seedy by-ways of the cyber world, determined to massage their sick egos by passing off, onto the frazzled and isolated gullible, their deceptively simple but poisonous fantasies. We should give them the widest of berths. If we don't engage our powers of reason, we run the risk of becoming prey to some seriously deranged notions.

Then we could find 2021 is no better, and perhaps a great deal worse, than 2020.

25 February 2021

Rabbit Holes for Children

Holding fast to a conspiracy theory has been compared to falling down a rabbit hole. Such a rabbit hole is a portal to an alternative universe, in which the realities of our everyday life no longer apply. The earth may be flat, Covid may be a conspiracy put about by the deep state, and elites may lust for children's blood.

These days, when we talk about a rabbit hole, we usually have in mind a gullible *adult* person as the one falling into it. But bear in mind that Lewis Carroll, who coined the phrase in the 19th century, imagined it was a *child* – Alice – falling down the rabbit hole. One built by an actual rabbit. Therein, Alice – true enough – found an alternative universe, but it was one populated by mad hatters, tea parties, and queens intent on chopping off heads.

What of present-day rabbit holes, the ones that lead to a world of contemporary fictions? Can children fall victim to these? Of course they can and, if you have children of your own, or even if you don't, you should be worried about this possibility. These holes are not built by rabbits. They are built by shady operators to be found on YouTube and other social media. These operators are child abusers. Their abuse is not usually physical or sexual. They are after minds not bodies.

The mind of a young child is a miracle of sorts, a thing to be held in great awe. It is a blank slate. A mind whose view of the world is totally objective, impartial, and unprejudiced. And impressionable. Early childhood is a state none of us (sadly) will ever visit again, because the process of living life consists of laying down a myriad set of predispositions – our own personal prejudices – which are very difficult to avoid or erase. Our slate is no longer blank. It has been written on many times over to the extent you can't see the slate anymore for the chalk. It's difficult to write anything new on such a slate.

So, who gets to write on the blank slate of a young child's mind? The Jesuits have famously said, 'Give me a child to the age of seven … '. In most instances, though, it's not religious figures that will write first. It's most likely to be the child's parents. Are they qualified to do so? That is doubtful. New-born children don't come with a user manual for parents. They, the parents, are obliged (mostly) to fly blind. But, to borrow Churchill's words on the subject of democracy as a method of government, parenthood is probably the least worst option for the guidance of young children.

Then, hot on the heels of the parents, will come those scum-of-the earth who would confound the minds of young children for no better reason than that they can. Like buzzards, they are found everywhere they scent opportunity. They have found that social media provide the ideal channels they need for the pernicious grooming of young minds. And those who are bent on such grooming will have made it their business to learn exactly how to talk convincingly to children. It is in their perceived interests to sound very plausible to the young.

What might they talk about? Any pet gripe they might have. Posing as an alternative reality. Nay, as the *only* reality.

The earth is flat. Vegans are evil. Greenies are evil. Scientists are evil. The government is evil. Don't allow yourself to be vaccinated. Covid is a fake. Don't do that or you'll go blind. Forget your parents and teachers, just believe *me*. Dire consequences are out there for those who stray from the path *I* prescribe.

Any rabbit-hole of an idea you can think of, no matter how low or what its odour, is out there seeking to impress itself on blank slates.

Children are endlessly intrigued by YouTube and the like. But, parents be warned. It will most likely achieve nothing if a parent tries to take control or prohibit their child's use of something as ubiquitous or as tempting as social media. Young children are likely to be more savvy about these things than are their parents and will find a way to carry on their activities clandestinely. Besides, not everything on social media is so poisonous.

So what can be done? I believe the answer is education. From an early age, give children the critical skills to form their own judgment. To evaluate opinions based on where those opinions are coming from. To train the blowtorch of logic on issues they stumble across in their travels.

Too difficult? Of course, its not easy. But the stakes are too high for us just to sit back and do nothing. Be part of the solution.

Look at the success of programs aimed at educating children

about sexual predation. Most children these days know what sexual molestation is and have acquired some rudimentary capacity for dealing with potential molesters. The battle is not won yet. But I like to hope it's on track to win.

Children are learning to have the ultimate say as regards ownership of their bodies. Equally, they should learn that their minds are exclusively theirs to manage.

1 April 2021

A Shot Across the Bow?

This is a vibrant liberal democracy. Not far from here, such marches, even now, are being met with bullets – but not here in this country. This is a triumph of democracy when we see these things take place.

- Scott Morrison, March 2021

Would you make a comparison between a hawk and a handsaw? Or between the stool on which you sit and the stool of a hairy-nosed wombat? Hardly, I suspect. There is no point of overlap within each pair of items which would make a comparison meaningful. Think of a Venn diagram. Only when there is such an overlap can a sensible comparison be made.

Scott Morrison, Prime Minister of Australia, *is* prepared to make a comparison between these two items:

(1) the recent demonstrations, peaceful and far too effective for his comfort, highlighting discrimination against women by the 'boy's club', particularly in Canberra, and

(2) the demonstrations in Myanmar that have, as we all know, been met with live rounds.

There *is* a point of overlap here, maybe more than one, to enable the comparison to be made. *I* can see the comparison. So, I suspect, can *you*. To get from one to the other, just add bullets.

But *why* would Morrison want to go public with such an inflammatory comparison in the first place?

Is it a warning? A shot across the bow? A subtle threat? A gentle hint that we should not step 'out of line'?

I can't be 100% sure he meant *any* of these things. But if he *did* mean even one of them, it is disgraceful behavior on his part. It undermines completely his follow-up words about 'triumph of democracy'.

I think it is a pity nobody with any real clout asked him for clarification on this point. Of course, he would have denied that he meant to play bully-boy but, at least, he would have been pulled into line. He would have been obliged to watch his words next time around.

As it stands, he may now feel emboldened.

What about the protest movements themselves? I have great sympathy for the women whose belittlement and abuse, some of it within the precincts of our seat of government, brought out so many all over Australia in support of their cause. And I am in awe of those unimaginably brave people in Myanmar standing up against a brutal military regime.

Who wouldn't share my sympathies with these people?

15 April 2021

Education Start to Finnish

[Photo courtesy of The Guardian]

If you have been reading my blogs over the years, you will be aware that one of my pet subjects is that of education, particularly education in critical thinking skills. Such skills have become especially important in these deceitful 20s, with so much wilful misinformation being put about in the mainstream media (especially in the Murdoch press) and on social media platforms.

Critical thinking skills enable one to assess the information one receives, and to form judgments about what is true, what is misleading, and what are outright lies. And (see my recent blog about rabbit holes) these skills are at least as important for children to acquire as they are for adults to acquire.

My personal skills in regard to critical thinking did not come about in any meaningful way until I reached year 12, at which stage my then English teacher, George Gibson, took it on as a crusade. George, perhaps, set too much store by crusades. He retired from teaching to become a missionary in Papua New Guinea, after which I never heard from him again. Possibly he came to a bad end.

George was the best teacher I ever had. The skills he imparted to me have stayed with me through life. I just wish I could have acquired these skills earlier.

In Finland, for example, the education system endeavors to impart such skills from kindergarten onwards. All power to them, I say.

Why should this quest have fallen to Finland to pursue? How is it they have come to lead the world in this respect? And will their shoulders prove broad enough?

Well, this small country of long bleak winters has of recent times been gaining a reputation for enlightened thinking *generally* when it comes to education. Finns would assert, moreover, that since they share a significant land border with another country, Russia, that has been fast gaining a much more dubious reputation – as a disseminator of misleading if not outright subversive information – they should inoculate their population from an early age against fake news.

Fake news? Educators in Finland prefer not to use this term. They like to classify suspect information as **misinformation** (mistakes), **disinformation** (lies & hoaxs), and **malinformation** (gossip). They claim kids relate to this classification better than to the blanket term, 'fake news'.

I'd like to quote a prominent Finnish educator on this subject:

> *'Kids today don't read papers or watch TV news … they don't look for news, they stumble across it, on WhatsApp, YouTube, Instagram, Snapchat … or more precisely, an algorithm selects it, just for them. They must be able to approach it critically. Not cynically – we don't want them to think everyone lies – but critically.'*

Would to God adults here could develop this critical thinking skill. Or is it a matter of old dogs and new tricks? Perhaps there is hope for future adults if early education, in *this* country, is geared up to impart these vital skills.

29 April 2021

Don't Be Corralled

Many of us like to be corralled. It feels safe. The safety of numbers. We – the willing sheep – are all in it – the corral – together. How good is that?

But is it really so good? I'd suggest, it depends on the motives of the person doing the corralling.

When medical experts corral us into getting the Covid vaccine, they are for the most part doing it for what the evidence tells them is our greater good. Our greater good, many of them will tell us, is herd immunity, the Holy Grail that will enable us to open up business, borders, and all the other things we have had to shut down to an extent during this terrible pandemic.

I go along with this sort of corral. I believe it is in my best interests, and will also serve the greater good.

But when it is a populist Prime Minister who tries to corral us, this is not necessarily being done for our greater good, but instead (primarily if not entirely) because he believes it will boost his chances of being re-elected. So, perhaps it is time we stopped, thought, and asked the question, Should we consent to be corralled by such a person, and is it in our best interests?

I am an iconoclast. My first instinct has always been to avoid corral. I like to think first and *only then* consent to be corralled. Or, more likely, not consent. I do *not* consent to Mr Morrison's presumptuous attempts to corrall me.

Perhaps this instinct of mine, to resist corralling, harks back to a vivid experience I had as a five-year-old (or thereabouts), and which has left an impression on me to last a lifetime.

My experience back then took the form of an oft recurring nightmare – recurring ones are the worst sort – in the course of which I would find myself corralled within a prescribed area of Australian bush whose perimeter was a ring of dead animals. The awful implication in my bad dream was that, should I try to cross that perimeter, I would myself become one of those dead animals. For weeks on end, I was afraid to go to sleep, because I knew I'd find myself back in that deadly corral.

Then, as an adult in the 1970s, I saw on screen for the first time a film, *The Exterminating Angel*, by Spanish film director Luis Bunuel. It blew my mind. For several days afterwards I walked around in a daze. Why? Can you imagine? If you've seen the film, you should be able to figure out why.

I was dazed because, in its essence, *The Exterminating Angel* mirrors my recurring dream. It was big time *deja vu* for me. In the film, a group of privileged people find themselves, in the course of a dinner party, unable to leave the confines of their hosts' apartment. In my dream, I am similarly trapped in my small area of Ozzie scrub.

No other film I have seen has left such a profound impression on me as this one did.

I have discussed *The Exterminating Angel*, and its particular significance for me, in one of my earlier blogs, and earlier in this anthology. You can find this blog on my webpage at **https://terrydeague.com**, or just flip back a few pages.

And I have made the theme of entrapment in a small space central to my latest novel. Naturally, the person who finds himself trapped inside 'The Space' becomes known as 'The Spaceman'. So, *The Spaceman* is the title of my new novel. And, despite its dystopian credentials, the novel is, to an extent, autobiographical. I have used my bad dream as its driving force.

When will it become available? Right now, I am in the process of finding a publisher for it. It *shall* be published, even if I have to do it myself. I will keep you informed via my blogs which, of course, may be found on **https://terrydeague.com**.

In the meantime, I have two pieces of advice for you: (1) don't go out in the woods today, and (2) don't consent lightly to your own corral.

20 May 2021

Where to Now?

So, fourteen months or so on, where are we? The pandemic has certainly turned our lives upside down. Everybody's experience of it is a little different. So let me concentrate here on mine.

I live in one of the more fortunate countries in the world. Perhaps you do too. Thanks to the timely action of our State Governments, of both political persuasions, we are in a safe space as regards Covid. Touch wood. It's not over till the fat lady sings. Things could still go pear shaped from this point, particularly if (1) we don't all get vaccinated asap, and/or (2) our quarantine system turns out to be unfit for purpose.

Mr Morrison, our Prime Minister, likes to say that 99% – I think that's his figure – of quarantines have been successful. This may be true, but it is the wrong statistic to be looking at in the circumstances of a pandemic. The 1% of failures, small though it may seem, is what matters. That 1% has lead to upwards of twenty instances of lock-down, including the very ugly one that went on to be the 'second wave' in Victoria mid 2020. Day by day, it's becoming apparent that hotel quarantine will *not* cut the mustard, and that dedicated quarantine facilities with lots of fresh air and open space will be required.

So, how should I react given this is how things stand? Perhaps I am being excessively cautious, but I am not at all inclined to leave Queensland yet. I don't want to find myself unable to return home from whatever foreign country or State of Australia I might choose to visit. We've seen how the Australian Government chooses to treat its own citizens trapped overseas.

Don't misunderstand me. There are countries in south-east and east Asia I would dearly love to visit, among them Japan, Singapore, Vietnam, and Taiwan. But even if bubbles were to open to them tomorrow, as one has recently for New Zealand, I would not rush out and book tickets. I know it doesn't sound at all charitable, but I would let other less cautious people test the waters for me. I would leave it for at least a year to see how the land lay, leaving – in the meantime – others to take the risks.

I'm not even inclined yet to visit other States. Queensland, where I live, is a very large State, and I haven't yet visited every part of it. And there are parts of it I could visit again, again, and again. I mean Winton, the Atherton Tablelands, the Daintree, Eungella, Lamington, and certain other very special places.

So, I will set out on another Queensland road trip with my partner, Janet. I have prepared an itinerary and started making the bookings already. We will be away from 26 July to 1 Sept. In some places, advance bookings are unnecessary but I'll make them anyway where I can. In other places, we won't get accommodation without an advance booking. Winton is an example, where, even 3 months in advance, I had to settle for my 4th choice of accommodation.

There is a wonderful feeling I get when, having set out on a substantial road trip, I cruise the outback roads with few distractions to get in the way of the natural attributes of the countryside. The air, clean and dry, is about as healthy as air can get. The landscape is mostly as flat as a plate. The sky is clear blue with, perhaps, the tiniest hint of cloud should you look hard. The people are utterly disarming, and in no way tricky, as city people can sometimes be.

Hell. I can't wait to set out. Bring it on.

17 June 2021

Winter Ambience

Keppel Sands beach, winter 2019

This is the view I get typically in the winter months looking east from my front verandah. The tide is out. The sky is clear. The sun is setting. The pastel swathes of iridescent sea in shades of blue and pink is a sight to take the breath away. These are winter colours.

The islands, of which eighteen or nineteen can be seen if you choose the right vantage point, are like candles, first lit up, and then snuffed out, as the sun sinks in the western sky. Under certain conditions, some of the islands can appear to float above the horizon, an effect caused by refraction of light through atmospheric layers of differing density. It is magical to see.

Sometimes, I spot a group of pelicans cavorting on the shoreline, or an elegant long-legged long-necked white bird – an egret I understand – stalking its prey in the sand there. More often than not, there will be a family of shy oystercatchers, black with bright red bills, doing likewise. Sea eagles soar overhead, the adults teaching their young how to fly, and how to plunge to sea level when a meal is in the offing. The wonderful birds here know me. They have seen me before as I have seen them.

Walking or gentle jogging on the soft sand is something I try to do every day. At a certain point, I sit down on an obliging rock and engage my senses. I identify the four buoys that guide tinnies through the safe channel between sandbars. Sometimes, I watch as one such tinny, just a white dot at first, comes over the horizon, taking the path suggested by these buoys until, adjacent to me, its occupant cuts the motor and throws a line over the side.

I haven't the patience to be a fisher. But, on one occasion, my partner, Janet, waded into the sea toting nothing more than a hand-line with some prawns for bait, and came out within thirty minutes holding up three winter whiting. Delicious for breakfast.

Sitting on my verandah, or on my obliging rock, I strain my ears. Sometimes, I hear human voices from a prodigious distance away. It is like being in one of those ancient Greek amphitheatres where you can whisper and yet still be heard over the other side of the stadium. Privacy can be impossible on the beach here on a clear still winter's day.

When there are no people or tinnies about, I hear something folk in cities never get to hear. Silence. It is a rare and special music conducive to a miraculous calm and to a life-affirming peace. If there is a breeze, I may get to hear the rustle of broad flat leaves or, best of all, the mysterious murmuring that happens when wind passes through the fine tendrils of a casuarina tree. There are plenty of casuarinas along the beach. The photo above has some good specimens in its foreground.

The temperature was 5 C at 6 a.m. this morning. It can be difficult sometimes rousing oneself from a warm and cozy bed at this time of year. But the temperature rose to 22 C by 2 p.m. and now, at 3 p.m., it is a fine sunny day. When it gets to 4 p.m. or soon after, the view from my verandah will start, should nature oblige, to look something like the photo above.

But it's time now for me to get on with my gentle jog.

22 July 2021

Three Bollards Outside My House

What's so exciting about that? Just three bollards out of treated pine? Nothing to see here.

But, recently, they were the scene of a stand-off of breathtaking effrontery involving some of the local bird-life, a stand-off worthy of inclusion in a David Attenborough documentary. Had I taken a video of the incident, it would have surely gone viral on social media.

A picture is reportedly worth a thousand words but, alas, I have no pictures. So you'll just have to make do with my words instead. And a tad of your visual imagination.

A large kookaburra, reputedly king of the bush, positioned himself/herself proudly on top of the centre bollard. Within minutes, a pair of butcher birds, each about half the size of the kookaburra, took over the bollards on each side. They glared at the kookaburra, who looked nervously at one butcher bird, then at the other, feeling himself/herself surrounded, capable of attack from either direction.

Then, in miraculous synchrony, a thing of great wonder, the butcher birds made their move. In a trice, they had swapped places. Their trajectories were opposing arcs, as of low-flying missiles. The kookaburra would undoubtedly have felt the breeze – and not a benign one – from their flapping wings on his/her ears. At the conclusion of this slick manoeuvre by the butcher birds, the kookaburra was still perched on the central bollard with a threat from each side, but with the positions of his/her attackers reversed.

The kookaburra, flummoxed, took quick nervous peeks to each side. The butcher birds glared back.

Then, to my delight and to the kookaburra's consternation, the butcher birds repeated the manoeuvre, quickly and gracefully. They swapped places again. The kookaburra shot nervous glances to each side. The butcher birds just glared.

The butcher birds did their trick a third time. Now the kookaburra had had enough. Intimidated, he/she hopped down to the base of the centre bollard, conceding defeat. The butcher birds glared down from a height with disdain.

One of the butcher birds then flew away. I imagined he/she in mid-flight saying to the one remaining, 'We've got this guy's measure now. You don't need me. From here on, you can handle the situation on your own.'

This remaining butcher bird continued to glare down at his/her quarry. Finally, the kookaburra shut up shop. He/she flew away to a position beneath dense bushes in my front yard, humiliated, but safe now from the perceived threat of aerial attack.

After a moment or two, the remaining butcher bird took off. Mission accomplished. Dominance established. Territory no longer in dispute.

Butcher birds, though highly intelligent, are as ruthless as their name suggests. They clearly know how to behave cooperatively. They are the orcas of the air, and their white-on-black colouring testifies to this. They have even learnt how to make humans, such as me, do their bidding. But that is another story for a future moment when I get around to telling it.

Finally, I should add that butcher birds have a most beautiful song, arguably the most attractive in the entire avian world. For tunefulness, their song is on a par with the iconic warble of the Australian magpie. I can't quite make up my mind which I prefer. By contrast, the raucous laugh of the kookaburra, irresistible though it may be, could not be described as melodious.

Pity the poor kookaburra. Nothing here to laugh about.

9 September 2021

Animals

The Gulf of Carpentaria is about as outback as you can get in Australia. We are just back from there after an eventful road trip. Janet has dubbed it 'the wild west without the guns'.

Take an example.

We rocked up to the Burketown pub for an evening meal. The new pub. The old one didn't survive the arson attack in 2012.

Inside the bar area, things were as rowdy as rowdy can get. Impossibly noisy. It was wall-to-wall men, with three exceptions: Janet, the long-suffering barmaid, and a middle-aged woman with a prosthetic leg. Most of the men were missing their front teeth and/or had a broken nose. B'Jesus, it looked rough. It looked like a war zone or a casualty ward. Going by the talk around town, I figured the fights would have been about women and/or horses.

We ate outside, al fresco, where it was quiet, and the visuals included a glorious outback sunset. For our entertainment, a swarm of tens of thousands of fruit bats, blackening the sky, set out to look for their evening meal. No fights in this community as far as I could ascertain. They had a common mission with (I presumed) rewards for all in the end. They were not in competition as far as I could tell.

We ate great barramundi. I'm not sure what the fruit bats were able to find.

Take another example.

I refer you to the the notorious 'animal bar' at Karumba, a small town that sits right on the waters of the Gulf, a place where waves and salt-water crocodiles come ashore in roughly equal numbers. The animal bar, part of the Karumba Lodge Hotel Motel, first came to the world's attention in the lawless days before Karumba had a police station. Nowadays, with police in attendance, one might have assumed the animals had been tamed and the bar had lost its mojo. This was the line put about by the management of Karumba Lodge when it petitioned for the bar's unflattering name to be retired.

But, a week or two before we hit town, a patron of the bar had had his ear bitten off in situ. The animals were still ascendant. The name stayed.

I figured the disputes here would have been about women and prawning leases.

Take yet another example.

The Albion pub in Normanton, the best of three in the town, serves the best barramundi meal in the Gulf, and an eclectic variety of cold beers on tap. Here, Janet received a proposal of marriage from an old fart that, I assume, props up the bar in perpetuity. I wasn't present at the time. I was out on the patio. Had I been present, and feeling mischievous, I might have asked him what his bride price was.

Now let's be clear about it: Janet is an attractive woman, despite her years. I would say *because* of her years. But I couldn't help but feel that the gender ratio in these Gulf towns is heavily weighted towards males. And that this sets the tone for what passes for social activity in this neck of the woods. And accounts for the fights.

Now I have a problem.

When I was very much younger, and lived in Melbourne, we had a saying apropos of people who took an unnecessarily circuitous route from A to B. We would say, 'Oh, he/she went via the Gulf of Carpentaria.' For us, the Gulf epitomized remote out-of-the-way places. Now that, for Janet and I at any rate, the Gulf has been effectively demystified, how do we now describe someone who likes to take the scenic route?

As a person who went via Shangri La? Or the mountains of the moon?

30 Sept 2021

An Analogue World

Milk comes out of cows. Apples grow on trees. And everything you see outside your window is analogue. Analogue as opposed to digital.

The entire natural and physical world is analogue, except for the digital constructs we humans have created for our own convenience. We now run the risk of replacing much of our authentic analogue experience with fabricated digital formulations.

An example.

I've heard it said that some schools don't bother anymore to teach youngsters how to read an analogue clock. That's the one with a clock-face, a big hand, a little hand, and (where precision is thought to be necessary) a fast-moving second hand. Such clocks are, of course, found everywhere on earth. Most homes have at least one. Every main street has at least one. For town halls, they are a necessary part of the furniture.

… and who, I'd like to know, gave these self-styled educators the God-like power to affect the futures of their young charges adversely by withholding their access to such a useful item of knowledge as how to read an analogue clock? …

I remember – as a relative newcomer to the wide world – with an age then still in the single digits – struggling to come to grips with these arcane devices, viz. analogue clocks. I remember my teacher valiantly trying to help me (together with a class-full of other confounded kids) to get the hang of them. The problem was as difficult to master as was long division, or the extraction of square roots, terrors also to be found in the curriculum in those long gone days.

We were told that, for a time of 2 hrs 22 minutes, the big hand sits just beyond 2, and the little hand just beyond 4. It makes perfect sense now but, back then, it was far from intuitive. How much easier would it have been to read 2:22 from a digital clock? Why choose the hard way to do things?

I believe I have an answer for this. For a start, time doesn't progress in incremental steps. It runs continuously. The movement of the big and little hands force us to realize this. The digital clock makes sudden jumps from 2:22 to 2:23, then from 2:23 to 2:24, and so on. There can be nothing in between. This is *not* how time actually works. Not in *our* universe. Analogue clocks run smoothly, thereby simulating the steady flow of time, which is exactly the sort of time we all live in.

Just as important, analogue clocks give us glimpses back into the recent past and forward into the near future, whereas digital clocks are rooted implacably in the present. Imagine the two scenarios below:

I'm expected at the meeting in exactly 40 minutes. If it takes me 20 minutes to drive there, and if I want to allow myself 10 minutes for unexpected delays, I had better get my arse into gear pretty damn soon to be on time.

Or:

Their flight should have landed two and a quarter hours ago give or take. Allowing them an hour to get through airport formalities, and another hour on the coach, they should be pounding at my door any moment now.

You can trace these scenarios out on a clock face in real time as we construct them in our minds. We do it as a matter of course, perhaps unconsciously. It is useful to be able to do so.

You *cannot* trace them out on a digital display.

Time is not the only quantity that can be represented in digital or analogue form. There are many many others. Just take a look around you.

Temperature, for example, can be read from a liquid-in-glass device or from an electronic gizmo. In the case of the liquid rising or falling continuously in the glass tube, you can get a feel for the way temperature operates in the real world. The electronic gizmo gives you no such feel.

And consider these two scenarios:

The mercury tells me the temperature right now is 18 C. The maximum for the day is forecast to be 25 C. I am told the overnight minimum was 8 C.

Or:

In the middle of summer, we can expect quite a few uncomfortable days in the low 40s. And I seem to remember a day a few winters back when there were ice crusts on the puddles in the morning. The temperature must then have dropped below zero over the previous night.

Just try visualizing these scenarios on a digital display.

Let's not decry digital. We embraced it – in the first instance – for the convenience it offers us. It has a legitimate place in our lives. But the real world is not pixelated. It is 'smoothed out' so to speak. And analogue displays give invaluable insights into how things will be, could be, were, or might have been. Into how the real world operates. Kids should *not* be denied these crucial insights.

Yes, milk *does* come out of cows and, last time I looked, it comes in continuous streams from their udders. It *also* comes digitized for our convenience, bottled in half-litre, one-litre, or two-litre increments. But the original analogue source, viz. cows' udders, tells us worlds more about the product we are consuming. Once bottled, it could be anything under the sun.

Give the kids the break they deserve. Expose them to the analogue.

21 October 2021

Real Wealth

Tourist: Say, Ranger, these mountains you got here … they worth anything?

Ranger: They give life to the glaciers that sculpt this bay. They're also important to the indigenous Tlingit, whose heritage is born of this place.

Tourist: No, no. I'm talking about minerals and mining. I'm talking about real wealth.

Ranger: So am I.

This conversation is reputed to have happened some time recently at Glacier Bay in Alaska. See the above photo. And the

Tlingit – you may have guessed – are the first nation people who own the land and are owned by it.

There's a stark clash of cultures here. Perhaps we can imagine our very own Gina czarina Rinehart, in conversation with, say, Bob's your uncle Brown. That's assuming they'd ever be found in the same room together.

The mention of glaciers sets me drooling. I have never been to Alaska, but I *have* seen glaciers in New Zealand and in Antarctica. Those experiences were memorable. Of all the large scale miracles of nature to which we may if fortunate be exposed, and confining ourselves for the sake of argument strictly to the inanimate ones – soaring alpine peaks, vertiginous coastal cliff faces, tranquil lakes dissolving into distant horizons, the very ocean itself in its immensity and with all its attendant hazards – of all these miracles, glaciers thrill me the most.

Stand at the business end of a glacier, look at what is before you, and take it in. You are like an ant in its presence. Each cubic metre of ice weighs a tonne give or take. So how many tonnes of ice do you see there, impelled by relentless gravity, bearing down on you like a killer avalanche? Thankfully moving ever so slowly, dare I say at glacial speed? Not as many tonnes, perhaps, as there are grains of sand on a beach, or stars in the sky, but a frightful number just the same.

But let's have done with calculations. Let's just stand there and feel in our bones the mind-blowing magnitude of the stresses and strains experienced by the fabric of the surrounding terrain. Feel the ravishment of the glacial bed. Feel the torture that the weight of ice applies to mother earth herself. Feel awe in our bones, as we – spared for the time being – are made aware of our own insignificance in the presence of things vastly more powerful.

Nature can and will be both beautiful and violent at the same instant.

This is an awareness that can stay with us for the remainder of life. Who's life? Yours and mine.

Can you ever put a dollar value on such an experience? Is this not real wealth?

18 November 2021

The Spaceman

Yes. The galleys of my second book have arrived. This means the bound copy should follow in a matter of days, and then it should be available for sale soon after. Watch this space.

This is my photo of the front cover. The title may confuse you. Be assured, the tale I tell is very much rooted on mother earth. Sorry. No interstellar adventures here.

So, what *is* the book about? On the back cover of the galleys is a synopsis. I reproduce it here:

> *What will the next pandemic look like? And must it be viral in nature? The author's conjecture, in his latest novel, The Spaceman, is that it will be different this time around.*
>
> *The Space is a patch of turf in the Australian Alps. Should a person or any other living creature enter this Space, they cannot leave except as a corpse. So, if they want to continue living, they must accept indefinite confinement. Ray Cromwell, picture framer, is the first person to be trapped in this way. He is the world's first Spaceman.*
>
> *Because evidence suggests The Space has a propensity to replicate and spread like a virus, the Government feels an obligation to deal promptly with the situation. But – no surprises – its response is political, opportunistic, and self-seeking.*
>
> *Tania Chalmond, Ray's business partner and eventual lover, teams up with Marius Strangio, the guy on the ground charged with administering the Government's response. Their mission is to secure Ray's release, despite their having no idea where the threat is coming from or what the rules of play are. They succeed after a fashion. They get Ray out alive. But there are too many bad players in this game, and celebrations prove to be premature …*

No mainstream publisher would accept my book. I regard this as a compliment of sorts. The publishing industry in Australia is in a self-inflicted doldrums, having adopted as a guiding principle the notion of 'what will sell'. This means they'll by-and-large accept established authors, celebrities, and/or stuff with a lowest common denominator appeal to the general public. Is this a policy for getting high quality stuff on the shelves? Have things always been this way? Or is it a product of mercenary 21st century thinking?

So, guided by a small concern called BookPOD, operating out of the suburbs of Melbourne, I self-published. Here is the result. I promise you quality. Buy it and see.

9 December 2021

In Search of a Life Ethic

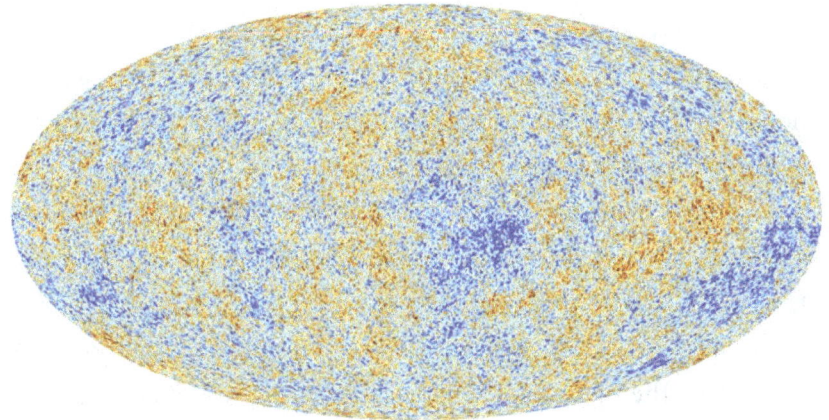

The Early Universe According to the Cosmic Microwave Background

Why should we concern ourselves with the big questions? Like, how did we get here? Like, what is the purpose of life? Like, what is our place in the universe? Why bother, when the answer, should you find one, will not put bread on your table, or secure you a roof over your head, or help to advance your career? Not directly anyway.

I maintain that it *is* important to think about the big questions. Vitally important. Over a lifetime of asking yourself the big questions, you can hope to develop a personal life ethic. And that ethic will be your guide to the big-picture issues that govern your life.

They're not called big questions for nothing.

Take the biggest question of all. The universe and how it got here.

I have a solid background in science, though not so much in

the area of cosmology. Nevertheless, I believe I have more than just a lay appreciation of this discipline. On this basis, I beg your permission to proceed.

Cosmologists agree that the universe came into existence some 13.8 billion years ago. At this juncture, a tiny sub-sub-atomic quantum fluctuation expanded out of all proportions, by a process known as cosmological inflation, to reach the size of the universe as we now know it. Let's get this in some sort of perspective. Based on what we can observe, the diameter of the universe is 28 billion light years give or take, but there is certainly going to be a lot more of it out there than what we observe.

If you want to regard the tiny quantum fluctuation as a 'wormhole', then an entire universe, including matter, energy, the laws of physics – even space and time themselves – gushed out through this wormhole in less than the blink of a sleepy eyelid. The phrase 'let her rip' comes to my mind. The question of what was there before this event is meaningless, because time itself had yet to come into being. Expressions like 'before this' and 'prior to this' make no sense in such a context.

Welcome to the big bang. And be thankful for it. We now have a place and a time in which to live. It is an unexpected gift of which we may or may not be worthy. Sadly, it seems to me, some of us are dragging the chain.

Quantum fluctuations are notoriously random, like a throw of dice. The particular random state, in which this fluctuation found itself at the time the big bang entered the fray, was frozen in place, just like our mothers were fond of telling us would happen if we pulled faces when the wind changed direction. This freezing-in-place accounts for the 'lumpiness' of our universe, the lumps becoming the stuff of galaxies and the like, not insignificant lumps by any stretch of the imagination.

A mere 370,000 million years into its eventful life – the merest of trifles compared with its total age today – the universe looked like the picture above. You could almost imagine continents and oceans, but you'd be wrong. The blue bits are not water. They are the colder bits and, accordingly, they are the most dense. The matter in them would eventually clump together under the influence of gravity to form galaxies.

This stunning picture – the earliest map of our very own universe – has been constructed from what is known as the 'cosmic microwave background', which is nothing more than the (hitherto) unexplained static and hiss picked up by curious radio astronomers bent over their workbenches.

Now some people would say the pesky quantum fluctuation that started the ball rolling was, in fact, the finger of God. Let's assume, for argument's sake, that God exists. Then, from my knowledge of Him/Her, I would say that He/She is not an interventionist. He/She likes to keep His/Her fingers out of the pie which, in this case, means the universe. This is fortuitous. The universe has, over the years, proved itself perfectly capable of running itself.

The above explanation resonates with me. But I understand some people will nevertheless prefer the story of the finger of God. To these people I say, whatever floats your boat, as long as it can sit alongside the science without subverting it. I may be an atheist, but I've no interest in being a *proselytizing* atheist. Whatever life ethic you choose, whether it involves religion or not, is fine by me, as long as it respects science, gives you the perspective within which you may chart your own course, and makes you a better, kinder person at the end of the day.

These are the positive outcomes of a good life ethic.

And what if you don't see the relevance of a life ethic? What if you just choose to go with the flow? Let me quote William Blake, English poet in the 18th and 19th centuries: 'I must create my own system, or be enslaved by another man's.'

In other words, if you don't take responsibility for your own life, somebody else will. This is the fate of all those confused frightened angry people who, at the bidding of people with seriously bad intentions, have stumbled into a rabbit hole, and now see no option but to lash out at the world in these fraught pandemic times.

16 December 2021

My Revamped Webpage

Have a look at my revamped webpage (**https://terrydeague.com**), done for me by the incomparable Glen Hawksworth of Technology Penguin, who does this sort of thing for a living, so that I can make my wares, and in particular my new novel, The Spaceman, available to you, the general public.

The webpage looks awesome. It is based on the print seen in the photograph above.

Now, if you have read the synopsis to The Spaceman that I posted recently, you may wonder what Edmond Lavrate's print ('Gros Bonnets') from 19th Century France has to do with the dystopia from 21st Century Australia that I have envisioned in my novel. The primary theme in my novel could be described as entrapment by pandemic, a phenomenon with which we are (doubtless) all too familiar. But there is a secondary theme.

It is power and authority, as depicted by the hats those with authority choose to wear. The hat you wear defines your role and status in society. Without a hat, you have no authority and no role, to wit the goose. Or is it a gander?

And therein lies the rub. You, in the 21st century, won't need to be told that gender should not matter but, when it comes to the crunch, does. So, a little problem lurks here, a problem that apparently hasn't changed over the ages. All those depicted in Lavrate's incisive print are men.

That would appear to have been the case in French villages in the 19th C, and it is clearly the case in our global village of the 21st C. The glass ceiling is alive and well.

Enter the female character, Tania Chalmond, in my novel. Given the circumstances, she is the person bringing the most heft to bear on events.

Are you intrigued? Are you sold? Then you must buy my book.

17 March 2022

My Friend, Vlad

Vlad. My old mate. My path has crossed yours several times. I must be one of the few Australians who can boast this. Though I never actually got to shake hands with you or anything like that, I *have* come across your trail on occasion. Rather like small critters such as ants or beetles might accidentally stumble on, and become mired in, the slimy path left by a snail.

Sorry, Vlad. That wasn't very nice, was it? Hold on a tick while I come up with a more flattering metaphor for you. Try this: rather like a small bird caught up in the wake produced on that memorable occasion which had you flying with Siberian cranes. Does that suit your ego better?

You won't remember me, Vlad. You almost certainly didn't even notice me. But, Vlad, I certainly remember you. The events to which I refer herein took place early in the 21st century when, on more than one occasion, I visited your home city of St Petersburg, partly because I like the place – what's not to like? – and partly because I wanted to further my studies in Russian language. I had previously studied Russian at university here in Oz and, finding its cadence and sonority rather attractive to the ear, decided to pursue it further. Strangely, the turbulent history of your country in the 20th and 21st centuries is not reflected in this gentle and mellow language.

To this end, I attended classes in Russian language in your beautiful city. Regrettably, I was never able to become fluent. But I'm proud to say I did get to read *Kapitanskaya Dochka* in the original Russian, with a dictionary beside me of course. Vlad, that's a novel by Alexander Pushkin, also a one-time resident of your city. As you would know.

And in St Petersburg is where our paths crossed. Mine and yours, Vlad.

The first occasion was in August 2000 when, only three months prior, a vodka soaked but democratically elected Boris Yeltsin handed over the reins of the Presidency to you. Remember that, Vlad? It was a big moment for you, and you were to take full advantage of it.

You'd also remember that things went pear shaped almost from the get go. Soon after my arrival, one of your nuclear submarines, the Kursk, had the audacity to stay stubbornly below the surface while you were at a holiday resort in Sochi. You took your own good time getting back on deck. When you *did* get back, you had a perfectly valid excuse for your indifference. Something to the effect that non-experts would only get in the way of rescue efforts. In any event, none of the crew survived, and you were castigated by some ungrateful dudes for your lack of empathy with their loved ones.

It all puts me in mind of something that recently beset our own Prime Minister here in Australia when he reluctantly came back from a holiday in Hawaii because much of the country was in flames. He was reported as having said, 'I don't hold a hose.' And he went on from there to deliver a masterclass in lack of empathy.

I felt really sorry for you back then, Vlad. I remember thinking, 'Poor devil. He won't survive this one.' But you proved me wrong, didn't you?

You have shown how it can be done. Perhaps there is yet some hope for our own Prime Minister.

My next visit was in the northern summer of 2003. This was a time of great celebration in St Petersburg. It was the 300th anniversary of the founding of the city. I was ready to join in the festivities in between taking some more classes in Russian language. But, Vlad, I was labouring under a misconception. You never intended the festivities to be for the pleasure of the common folk. This was only ever going to be an event for you to showcase and advance your own power.

So it happened that, as I strolled along a footpath in central St Petersburg – essentially minding my own business – enjoying the weak sunshine – a menacing motorcade of limousines with motorcycle escorts roared recklessly round a corner. My impression at this moment was that the drivers were under instructions to treat their vehicles as if they were weapons. Had I been jaywalking, I swear I would have been road-kill. Vlad, I'm pretty sure you would have been sitting back inside one of those vehicles, your backside making its decisive impression in the soft leather upholstery. Of course, I couldn't tell with absolute certainty that it was you, because all the occupants were behind tinted glass. But, on the balance of probabilities, I'd say it was highly likely you were there. A little jaunt like this with those dearest to your heart – your rich and powerful mates – is just the sort of caper one might expect of you.

Vlad! Vlad! A matter of mere metres separated us, Vlad. This was, unfortunately, as close as I would ever get to you. But so *very* close. You were dispensing shock and awe to the masses as is your wont and, at the same time, you were gathering brownie points from those that really mattered in your cloistered world.

Fast forward a day or two, Vlad, and you'll find me presuming to take advantage of the hospitality you famously extend to those you favour, through the carefully coordinated program of events you have authorized for the festivities. In the small but beautiful backstreets of this fabulous city of Peter the Great, I came across a small string ensemble preparing to give a recital. I sat down. The conductor raised his baton and, at his behest, gentle music flowed.

But not for long.

Suddenly, a blast of piped and raucous music sounded from loudspeakers strategically placed in a nearby public square. This cacophony drowned out the delicate performance I had been enjoying. The hapless conductor hung in there for a while but, unable to compete with this obscene amount of noise, eventually chose to point his baton in its direction, and pretend to conduct along with it it. The look on his face, Vlad, was a real picture. It was a look of ironic resignation. He had seen all this before.

(A question for you here , Vlad. The specific piece of piped music that so rudely interrupted all other proceedings was, I believe, *Marche Slave* by Pyotr Ilyich Tchaikovsky. This piece was originally intended to commemorate the intervention of Russian forces in the Serbian-Ottoman war of 1876. Was this choice deliberate on the part of your cronies and, if so, does it prophesy present day – and possible future – interventions?)

Just a few days later came the grand parade down Nevsky Prospect, highlight of the festivities celebrating the 300th birthday of the fair city. The weather was perfect for the occasion. Excitement was in the air. Masses of ordinary Russians were vying for the best vantage points.

Then – on your instructions, Vlad, I presume – the *politzaya* moved in, and all these starry-eyed folk – patriots to the last person – were cleared out.

Tables were set up, then the tables were laid. And then, as if from thin air, the *apparatchiki* – paying customers – were moved in. Soon their bums – and those of their wives, mistresses, girl friends, or whatever – were on seats. These clowns were busy feeding their faces, swilling vodka, and watching the parade through a communal alcoholic haze. Somewhere beyond them, somewhere that the ordinary folk and I couldn't see, that parade was happening.

Thank you from me, Vlad, for a most illuminating spectacle.

Vlad, you knew what you were doing, didn't you? Two decades later, this sort of caper now sees you in the best of stead. The general public may be fickle but, as the situation stands today, the same *apparatchiki* you cultivated back then, and who now occupy positions of power at your decree, would swear black was white if you told them it was so. You have them by the short and curlies, Vlad. Isn't this the very definition of leadership?

Fast forward a few years, and I am in St Petersburg once more for language lessons. On the weekend, I take a train to a region just beyond the outskirts, to visit one of the sumptuous palaces built back in Tsarist days. The train is full of ordinary Russians with, I presume, a recreational purpose in mind. Just like me.

We pass a station on the way. Its platform is filled with Roma – men, women, and children distinguishable as Roma by their colourful costumes – carrying with them what looks like it could be all their worldly possessions. When I say the platform is filled, I mean there isn't room to put a toothpick down. All the Russian passengers clutch instinctively at their wallets and their faces all drop. I can read the question in their mind: 'The train's not planning to stop here, is it?'

Roma – gypsies – have the capacity to put the fear of God into ordinary Russians. And, on this ill-fated platform, it is not just a handful of Roma. What we see here is a massive horde of their ilk. A Roma convention, perhaps? Many a time, when Roma are on the prowl, ordinary Russians, like those on this train, have seen their wallets and watches disappear before their eyes as if by magic.

To the immense relief of all on board, the train doesn't stop at this station. But the incident sets me wondering. What are all those Roma doing crowded into the one small space, looking for all the world like they are about to be victims of a final solution? Are they being herded? Could there be guards set at the station's exit to prevent them fleeing? All things considered, Vlad, what I'm witnessing has a bad smell and, though I can't for the life of me figure out why, something about this stench puts me in mind of you.

But, Vlad, one thing that can be said in your favour is you don't discriminate. Not against Roma. Not against Jews. Not against gays. Not even against Pussy Riot. Not even against those pesky

Ukrainians. When it comes to the crunch, Vlad, they are all much of a muchness to you.

The focus of your contempt, Vlad, is ordinary people in general. They are in your way and, as such, are expendable trash, beneath your dignity to even acknowledge.

21 April 2022

Karl Duldig

Karl Duldig was my art teacher at secondary school. Art was not a subject I took particularly seriously. And I certainly didn't realize back then that Karl was an artist of some renown in the wider world.

The bronze sculpture shown above is by Karl. It is good. It is entitled '*Kore*'. The name, *kore*, has come to mean a high-class maiden, often from ancient Greece, draped elegantly, and with an austere attitude. Karl's *kore* stands in Central Park in the Melbourne suburb of East Malvern, a suburb in which Karl eventually was to settle.

Karl was born in Przemysl in Poland, the place to which many Ukrainian refugees are fleeing as we speak. My heart goes out to them.

At age 12, Karl moved to Vienna with his family. This is where he became interested in (among other things) sculpture. It is where he studied, developed skills in, and practiced this art form. He did so until the *Anschluss* – the annexation of Austria by the Nazis in 1938 – at which time he realized his Jewish ancestry could put him at peril.

So Karl fled with wife and child to Switzerland and, from there, somehow found his way to Singapore. After a short period practicing his trade in this totally new environment, he was deported to Australia as an enemy alien, and ended up in an internment camp in Tatura, near Shepparton in Victoria.

The war over, Karl acquired Australian citizenship, and set up shop once again, this time in Melbourne. To lend financial support to his artistic inclinations and to his family, he took a full-time job as Art Teacher in a private boy's school in Melbourne, a school I would describe politely as quirky, and not so politely as shithouse. That's where I met him, in my capacity as a young student at said school. A student (as I have already flagged) with no special enthusiasm for his subject.

Some of you would have experienced displacement in your lives, owing to flood, fire, foreclosure, or whatever. I commiserate. But, without wanting to belittle the traumatic consequences that doubtless befell those of you so unfortunate, I make the point that Karl's experiences would have included some very special indignities.

He would have left a comfortable environment in a tearing hurry, with nothing more than a couple of suitcases. He would have left for no better reason than an accident of birth, a funny accent, and a foreign name. Invariably, he would have had to master a new language in his new environment. For most of us, living a comfortable life here in Australia, his experience is beyond the range of the imaginable. To get some sort of handle on it, to stand in his shoes so to speak, to know how he felt about the deal he was dealt, we would somehow have had to hijack his neuronal network for a period and assume it as our own.

Karl's indignities did not stop happening once he reached Melbourne. He was now captive to a cruel breed who knew how to dish them out with relish. That breed consisted of schoolboys barely out of short pants, of which – much to my shame – I was then one.

One of the games we liked to play was to press all the buttons of any teacher who showed what we regarded as weakness. Karl had plenty of such 'weaknesses'. He was ingenuous, sincere, conscientious, and foreign, so he played right into our hands. We were merciless in Karl's class, and made his life hell.

Karl even provided us the *materiel* that helped us play our games. There was stiff paper on which masterpieces could be created, but which served even better as paper planes. There were coloured paints that were intended to adorn said paper but also, as we were to demonstrate with alacrity, any presenting surface of our choice. There was clay to be sculpted, but which we preferred to use as ammunition.

The guy who mostly took charge of our unscheduled activity in these art classes was a vicious young twerp called Bernie Bancroft (not his real name). He was a choice piece of work if there ever was one, and I figured, correctly as things transpired, he would one day come to a bad end. He often led the charge against Karl and when he did we, like pack animals on the prowl, smelt blood and moved in for the kill.

Back then, I sometimes felt sorry for Karl, but could seldom resist the temptation to have fun with the gang at his expense.

Karl, realizing he could do nothing but grin and bear, was the stoic gentleman, but there was one occasion when he very nearly lost his cool. On that particular day, the project he had in mind for us was to draw spiders. We set to work.

Karl moved amongst us, peering over our shoulders at the banal efforts that flowed halfheartedly from our brushes and pencils, relieved at least to find we were not yet running amok. He smiled benignly at a succession of formless black blobs from which eight spindly straggles inevitably sprouted. We knew our spiders.

Then he came to Bernie. This classroom Philistine, ever seeking mischief, was adding the finishing touches to *his* drawing. What Karl saw over *his* shoulder was the representation of a tall glass containing a frothy beverage much coveted by those of us not yet habituated to alcohol. In Yankeeland, it was known as an ice-cream soda, but we in Oz, always adept at making absurd connections, had chosen to dub it a milk spider.

Karl baulked.

Zeess is not a spider, he said.

Zeess *is* a spider, said Bernie.

Karl raised his voice a notch.

Zeess is not a spider, he said.

Zeess *is* a spider, said Bernie.

Arms flailing desperately as if to ward off attack, Karl raised his voice another notch.

Zeess is not a spider, he said.

Zeess *is* a spider, said Bernie.

At some point in this fruitless exchange, Karl must have realized he couldn't win. He had met his match. His hands fell to his sides, and his reddening face quivered. The class broke into laughter, incapable of mitigation. I imagine Karl was wishing he was back in his beloved pre-war Vienna, or even Singapore. Or, indeed, anywhere else but here. Admitting defeat, he moved on. His demolition, courtesy of a classroom full of little shits, was complete.

I believe it was later that year when the school held an open day, to demonstrate (I assume) to the parents of its young charges, that its services were worth the money they were forking out. When it comes to open days, Art is a subject that, unlike say Mathematics or History, lends itself well to public display. Art is inclined to come into its own on such days.

I was flabbergasted to find one of my artworks was there for all the world to see.

Please give me leave to explain.

The project Karl had in mind for us, on a particular day some weeks prior to open day, was to draw a boxer. I guess he was motivated in his choice by an announcement our headmaster had made at school assembly a day or two earlier. Boxing, he announced, would now be available to us as a optional extra on sports afternoons. Go for it, he added. It's a gentleman's sport.

Sport, like Art, was not my bag at all. But I – some Johnnies might say I was a sporting girlie man – was appalled by the idea that clobbering someone around the head with padded fists could be considered sport. In my view it was barbarism. It was gentrified and authorized bullying. The Marquess of Queensberry notwithstanding, where was the sport in that? So, carrying my outrage into Art class, I decided to take Karl's project seriously. I would *not* join in the usual shenanigans, at Karl's expense, with

Bernie and the other pack animals. That could wait. Right now, I had more important things on my plate.

I set to work with uncharacteristic fervour. I was on a mission. As I applied pencils, pastels, and paints to the task Karl had set, feelings of revulsion gushed from some well deep inside me and poured out onto the sheet of art paper in front of me. The rudiments of a crude image formed there. In considerable abstraction, it consisted of a boxing ring with a male boxer inside, punch drunk and on the ropes. If I may say so myself, the poor devil was a sorry sight.

Not happy with my creation, I attacked it again and again with a coarse eraser, bruising the surface of the paper and exposing its fibres. This had the unintended effect of giving my work some texture. The boxer looked really roughed up and bloodied now. He was not a pretty sight at all. I imagined there would be cadavers that looked in better shape.

My passion spent, I looked it over and decided it was a mess. But Karl must have collected it afterwards and decided it had something. It gave me quite a shock to discover that, without my knowledge or permission, he had arranged for its display on open day. Of course, it wasn't alone. There was a smattering of other student art, beside which even my rudimentary effort looked good. Pickings were slim when it came to the portfolios of unmentionable brats.

Somebody must have pressed Karl to bring a sample of his own work for display, because there, amidst all the dross, was a sculpture by him out of baked clay, the size of a human baby, and I suspect about as fragile. Its subject was two wildcats fighting.

Like all of Karl's work, there was no way it would ever be described as static. This was no lifeless statuette, as inert as the clay it was made from. You would swear those wildcats were in vigorous motion, engaged as they were in their dance of death. Believe me, that's the impression it gave. Unequivocally.

Just have a look back at the photo of the *kore* he did, presented for your convenience above. Reflect meanwhile that *korai* are supposed to exude an ancient and austere dignity. Mortal humanity, assumedly, is way beneath them. But Karl's *kore is* human, full of voluptuous and unabashed life.

This was not the last time I was to see those incredible wildcats. Decades later, Karl dead for some years at this juncture, and my boxer drawing long gone to landfill, I visited his former home in East Malvern, converted into a museum now by his relatives and admirers. It was an an unassuming red-brick dwelling from the 1920s, typical of what you might find in the area.

There was an expansive back yard adorned by some of Karl's sculpted pieces nestled among the greenery as if they rightly belonged there. Which they did. And there was a studio, a later addition to the back of the house. This room, light and airy, show-pieced some of Karl's equipment. More than this, it housed a selection of his smaller art works.

Among them was his aggressive pair of wildcats. They jumped out at me, going for my jugular. Instantly, I was transported back in time to my schooldays. The grass I could smell was not the freshly cut lawn in the backyard of the late Karl Duldig, artist of some renown. It belonged to the sporting oval of my old school of somewhat less renown. Was this *deja vu* or was this *deja vu*?

I spoke to the woman who had greeted me at reception, Karl's granddaughter I believe. I told her I had been one of Karl's students at *that* school, and how we had treated him so very badly.

We knew, she said.

I ventured an apology for my part in our unconscionable games. Had Karl still been around, I would not have hesitated to deliver it directly to him. As it was, I can only hope and assume his granddaughter accepted it on Karl's behalf.

Some would say we should respect our elders. I would add the codicil: 'as long as they warrant it'.

Karl warranted it. Without a shadow of doubt.

5 May 2022

Art in the Outback

Is there art in the outback? Isn't that the place where rednecks and yokels abound? Couldn't expect much in the way of art from *that* crowd, could you?

Well, brace yourself for a surprise.

The photo above is of a community shelter in the main street of Hughenden in outback Queensland. Having made use of it several times during my forays with Janet into the outback in the last couple of years, I can vouch for its functionality, and would also like to make a case for its artistic merit. Those who accept the big-city definition of art may not be convinced. Ho hum, they might be inclined to say. Nothing to see here.

But the art produced by any given community, whether in city or country, will always tend to reflect what is foremost in the minds of that community.

Windmills are vital to the very existence of a town like Hughenden. Windmills, I venture to suggest, dominate the neural networks of all residents of this town whom, I might add in passing, I have found to my satisfaction will always be ready to extend a friendly hand to visitors. Windmills provide access to the water of the Great Artesian Basin, without whose water the town would not be on the map. Windmills are as critical as that. So, they will sooner or later make their presence felt in any art produced in the region. Hence the above.

Have a look at a road map of Queensland, and compare it with a road map of that other mammoth state, Western Australia. In the outback of Queensland, there are any number of small towns like Hughenden with populations not exceeding 10,000 people or thereabouts. By contrast, the map of Western Australia shows that, in the outback, towns of this size – of *any* size – are much less prevalent. WA is not blessed with a Great Artesian Basin.

The exception would be places like Kalgoorlie or the Pilbara, whose massive wealth in resources means that money *will* be spent delivering water to them by any means necessary. By hook or by crook. It is interesting to speculate what variety of art would blossom in such places. The chances are it would *not* involve windmills.

People in the big cities often fancy themselves as the ultimate arbiters of art. But art is more flexible than these people would have it.

All art counts. You can always learn something from it. Even in the outback.

26 May 2022

On the Flinty Path Alone

We all have a favorite poem. It might be a stylish Shakespeare sonnet with talk of anonymous love. Or those with a taste for the epic might prefer Dante's *Inferno* or Coleridge's *Rime of the Ancient Mariner*. For those who prefer something more local, it might be Banjo Patterson's *The Man from Snowy River*.

I have a few favourites. Top of the list has to be the soliloquy from *Hamlet*, written by Shakespeare to be spoken by Hamlet. It's the one that famously begins 'To be or not to be.' It tackles head-on and with great angst the existential issue of whether or not life is preferable to death. Even as I read it today, or hear the spoken words resounding in my head, it sends shivers down my spine. It is a masterpiece of conciseness and elegance.

Then there is the short poem *For Whom the Bell Tolls* by John Donne. Wonderful aphorisms about personal moral responsibility burst from every line. No need, though, to shy away from it, because – contrary to what one might expect – it's not especially preachy. Try the opener 'No man is an island' for size. Pity Donne didn't use gender-inclusive language, but I doubt his contemporaries in the 17th century would have been too concerned.

Then there is the amazing stuff by William Blake, such as 'Tyger Tyger, burning bright/In the forest of the night/etc.' Being more metaphorical in nature, it's not written in such direct language as the above two examples. And it grabs you. Reading Blake is a bit like viewing art by Salvador Dali, or should I perhaps say art by Blake himself. His art is almost as renowned as the words he put on paper.

Here is yet another example I came across only recently. It is by Mikhail Yuryevitch Lermontov, and is called *I Go Out on the Road Alone*. There are various translations of it from Russian to English, but the one I like best is the one I reproduce below. I cannot find the translator's name. Unknown and unknowable, he/she would appear to prefer anonymity.

In the original Russian, it rhymes. In English translation it doesn't, but I think the poem is none the worse for that.

So:

I Go Out on the Road Alone
by Mikhail Yuryevich Lermontov

Alone I set out on the road;
The flinty path is sparkling in the mist;
The night is still. The desert harks to God,
And star with star converses.

The vault is overwhelmed with solemn wonder
The earth in cobalt aura sleeps ...
Why do I feel so pained and troubled?
Why do I harbor hopes, regrets?

I see no hope in years to come,
Have no regrets for things gone by.
All that I seek is peace and freedom!
To lose myself in sleep!

But not the frozen slumber of the grave ...
I'd like eternal sleep to leave
My life force dozing in my breast
Gently with my breath to rise and fall;

By night and day, my hearing would be soothed
By voices sweet, singing to me of love.
And over me, forever green,
A dark oak tree would bend and rustle.

I ask myself, Where have I been all my life that I've only recently come across this little gem? Every time I read it, I am transported.

I first encountered it watching a recent doco on SBS called *Meeting Gorbachev*. Made by film director Werner Herzog, this doco has Herzog himself interviewing Mikhail Gorbachev, the last General Secretary of the USSR, and the man accredited with having presided over the demise of the Soviet Union.

In the interview, Gorbachev comes across as a most amenable person, exuding a great deal of warmth and humanity. He is not in any way like that pathetic paranoiac currently running the Russian Federation like it was his own fiefdom. In a classic of understatement, full of lament, Gorbachev makes it clear that he sees Putin as having thwarted the program he put in place before he resigned. He quotes from the inscription on the gravestone of an unnamed friend: 'We tried.'

Then, in a most moving moment, he launches into a recitation in Russian of Lermontov's poem. At the conclusion he pauses, then says softly, Da. Another pause. Then once again, Da.

What can I say?

This is a documentary you should watch.

21 July 2022

Winter Birds

Winter, we in Queensland are prone to say flippantly, was on a Tuesday this year. On this auspicious day of this year, i.e. the day winter chose to appropriate for its purposes, the maximum temperature fell a shade short of 18 C. In Tasmania or Victoria, such an outcome would sound positively balmy. But here, where the Tropic of Capricorn crosses the east coast of Australia, it is the deepest that winter shall usually get.

I love winter. It is my favorite season. Summer, by comparison, is a ruthless bully, bringing with it cyclones (a.k.a. hurricanes), electrical storms, floods, and unbearable humidity. Bringing with it any foul thing the elements can throw at us. Winter, on the other hand, is steady as she goes. It brings stability, a gentle coolness, pastel colours, and clear fresh air in which sound carries forever.

And birds.

Birds, for me, are a constant joy. I often wonder if they weren't put on earth just to jolly up our congenitally morose species. Here in Capricornia, if I am permitted to name just a few varieties, there are pelicans (as per the photo), sea eagles, oyster catchers, black cockatoos, tawny frogmouths, magpies, and butcher birds. And, of course, kookaburras, darling birds.

All seem to be glad it is winter.

Walking on the beach in late afternoon, with Janet's adult son for company, I (and he) sit ourselves down on an obliging rock to watch the tide come in, taking on the form of a flurry of turbulent wavelets. We are both dressed in identical black. A pair of seagulls watch us with the curiosity that seems innate in all birds.

The next afternoon, we repeat this routine. A pair of seagulls watch us as before.

Are they the same pair? Geoff asks.

How would we know? I reply.

And I imagine the seagulls having their own seagull conversation in which they discuss us humans.

Are they the same pair? says one.

How would we know? the other replies.

11 August 2022

A Valetudinarian's Journey

What the hell is a valetudinarian? you might well ask. Please read on. All will be revealed.

A week or so before we were due to set off on a road trip (our third in three years) to far western Queensland, Janet (my long-time partner) developed an ugly lesion on her left forearm. It was a lesion which would have had any Tom Dick or Harry thinking 'melanoma' in a trice. That's M-E-L-A-N-O-M-A for Pete's sake. Certainly I – with, admittedly, an unqualified eye – thought it was a likely melanoma. Her GP thought it was a likely melanoma. And, the very next day, her surgeon thought it was a likely melanoma.

The lesion was removed without delay, leaving an ugly scar,

almost ten centimetres long, replete with stitches and staples. It looked like a gigantic red centipede crawling up her arm.

In due course, the results of a biopsy came back to us. Voila. The lesion was benign. It was just a bruise that had gone feral. Them's the breaks.

Had we known, we could have saved ourselves time, money, and a lot of angst. But how could we have known? It might easily have been a real melanoma. In such cases as ours, so the thinking goes, it's always better to be safe than sorry.

So we set off on our road trip with Janet sporting a sore arm and a load of anxiety. Our plan was that the staples and stitches would be removed out west in the town of Charleville where, courtesy of the Queensland Government, and by all reports, there was a hospital and a clinic whose staff had the necessary skills.

From the outset, Janet was fretting. Should the wound be kept covered or exposed to the air? Would it heal over? When would it stop weeping? When would the redness subside? How often should the dressing be changed? When/if it did heal, what sort of scar would be left? Was it infected beyond hope? Her head was a nest of rats, all of them playing around with a single ball of thought: my poor arm, my poor arm, my poor arm …

The dreaded A word (A for Anxiety) haunted her to the extent that we were obliged to call in at government hospitals or health clinics at every wide place in the road we encountered to have the wound assessed. That's just the hospitals and clinics. I wont even bother to mention the pharmacies we visited.

As we progressed further and further west, we moved into increasingly remote territory. It seemed at times that we were moving inexorably away from the possibility of help if/when we required it. Just as wi-fi and mobile phone coverage were becoming increasingly dicey, so (we imagined) was competent medical service. Should we change our plans? Should we turn back?

First up was Goondiwindi, population 11,000. Here, we visited the hospital. The nurses and doctor seemed more concerned with Janet's pulse rate and blood pressure than they were with her arm. Her anxiety was sending her cardiac function all over the shop. On the basis of this, and not of her arm, the doctor wanted to admit her to the hospital. In the end, she released Janet with a course of antibiotics. But Janet was still anxious.

Next was Charleville, population 3,000. Here, the stitches and staples were removed without any fuss. I was somewhat surprised at the speed of response and the high degree of competence the nurses displayed. The 3,000 residents of Charleville, it seemed to me, were in excellent hands. But Janet was still anxious.

Next was Cunnamulla, population 1,200. We visited the hospital. Janet was in and out in no time at all, with a fresh script for a more powerful antibiotic, and a qualified assurance that the wound was progressing well. But Janet was still anxious.

Next was Thargomindah, population 270. A lovely little town. We visited the clinic. When Janet asked if it was safe to venture further west, i.e. to our ultimate and most westerly destination of Innamincka, one nurse quipped that the last people to die out there had been Burke and Wills in 1861. They (the nurses) did not seem to think her arm was a problem. But Janet was still anxious.

… for the benefit of those unfamiliar with Australian history, Robert O'Hara Burke and William John Wills led an expedition to cross the mostly uncharted continent from South to North and back. They were rookie explorers, and their incompetence was mind-blowing. Cooper Creek, where they drew their last breaths, was full of fish just waiting to jump onto a hook. Yet Burke and

Wills are today the most celebrated of Australia's inland explorers. Like the Gallipoli landing in WW1, Australians seem to love to glorify their abject failures …

Back to our road trip. And, while talking of roads, the photograph above gives you an idea of the terrain in and around Innamincka.

We reached Innamincka, permanent population 16. This place is so far west, we actually crossed a border into the state of South Australia to reach it. We stayed there two nights, and got to know all sixteen of the permanent residents. We were put up by Cooper Creek Homestay, comprised of a husband, wife, and two young children. This meant that a quarter of the permanent population were right there on our metaphorical doorstep.

When Janet told the wife (Allie) about her arm, Allie told Janet that a specialist dermatologist from Sydney had flown in via the Flying Doctor that very day, and was inviting appointments. Janet jumped at the chance.

So, the dermatologist inspected Janet's wound, declaring that it had healed up very nicely and was showing no sign of infection. From this point on, Janet's anxiety began to wane. Her inner valetudinarian was satisfied.

So as to never let a chance go by, I had my entire skin checked by the specialist for suspicious spots. I emerged with a clean bill of health as regards skin. I happened to mention to him that I thought Janet was a bit of a valetudinarian, and followed up by asking him if he knew what that word meant.

Oh yes, he replied.

But for your benefit, who may not know, I give you a definition. A valetudinarian is a person who is inordinately anxious about their health. I believe it derives from the days of the Romans, when military field hospitals were known as valetudinaria (singular: valetudinarium), and people who frequented them as … valetudinarians.

We are on our way east now and getting close to home. Here at Winton, Queensland, population 850, I feel the need to reflect on Janet's encounters, whilst on the road, with sundry latter-day valetudinaria and their staff. The quality of the medical care she received from them was exemplary across the board, despite the remoteness of the locations.

And how much did it cost us? Not a brass razoo.

Ask yourself this. In what other country of the world would top-notch medical services be provided to anyone in the wide brown land, no matter how far removed they are from the big smoke, with no questions asked, and at no cost? Provided to anyone who fronted up, even itinerant valetudinarians?

If we are the lucky country then, to an extent, we have made our own luck.

25 August 2022

This Man Is No Joke

Morrison always liked to portray himself as the jokey blokey. Thank providence he is now out of office, having lost at the ballot box. But now, his attempts while in office to undermine the Westminster System underpinning our democracy are coming to light. This is no joke.

I refer, of course, to his establishment, shrouded in as much secrecy as he could conjure up, of a shadow government where he, as 'president', got to control multiple important portfolios. Portfolios held already by the very ministers he had appointed, ministers who for the most part didn't even know they were being shadowed.

No. He is not, as he would have it, a jokey blokey. While in office, he was the worst prime minister of Australia in my living memory and, arguably, the worst in the history of Australia. Even out of office, he is proving himself a clear and present danger to our democracy.

So don't encourage him. Don't allow yourself to be manipulated. Don't laugh with him as he attempts to laugh away all his misdemeanors. Insist he be held to account for his outrageous behavior while in office.

We don't need to see the likes of him again this side of doomsday.

8 September 2022

CapriCon

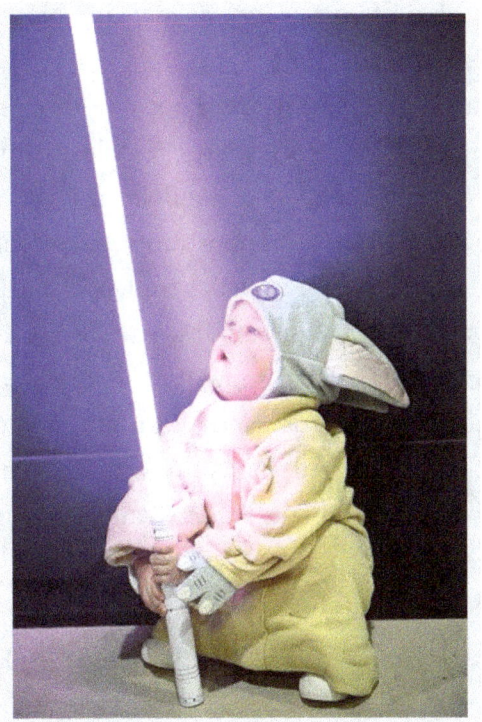

CapriCon is an event held at the Showgrounds in Rockhampton, Qld, each year late in August, but the show is more cultural than agricultural. That's not to say it doesn't have animals. This year, there were some charming baby goats, but they were billed as therapy animals not as potential blue-ribbon contenders.

CapriCon describes itself as 'the largest single-day pop culture convention in Central Queensland showcasing a wide spectrum of pop culture including comics, collectibles, cosplay, anime, medieval, gaming, art, steampunk, and more.' The 'more' apparently includes local literary accomplishments, because I was encouraged to set up a stall there (in 'author's alley') to promote my latest book, *The Spaceman*.

The area I was allotted was a mere 2m x 2m. Not to worry. How big, after all, is a book?

So, how was I to adorn my space, meagre though it might be? What props might I use to attract clientele to my little patch? Well, I called on a friend of mine, Paul, from two doors down the road. And he jumped at the opportunity to exercise his artistic bent in my interests. Which is just as well, because I was clueless.

So, Paul went at it like a bull at a gate. He created a make-believe Space, complete with snow out of shredded paper, a red line which one must not cross, and a sign propped up by an easel saying 'Abandon Hope All Ye Who Enter Here'. And much more. If you've read my book, which Paul has, you'll know the significance of these props.

Oh, one more thing. He mocked up a top hat for me to wear. As you would be aware from reading my book, funny hats is a sub-theme in the scenario of *The Spaceman*.

We set everything up *in situ* on the afternoon prior to the event. Then, from 7 a.m. the next day, it was all systems go. I sat at my card table in my top hat spruiking my book, while Janet sat beside me playing cashier, with a float of fives and twenties. Nothing high tech here. No eftpos. Nothing but the folding stuff.

And the carnival was in play all around us. What a carnival it was. Candy for the eye. There were a minority of really original hand-made costumes, usually period efforts, which I'm obliged to applaud. Less laudable, but entertaining nonetheless, was the profusion of Darth Vaders wielding Jedi swords, or characters out of *Game of Thrones*. The parade of people sporting their alternative realities was theatre enough even if, perchance, I didn't get to sell a single book. The costume hire people in Rockhampton must have really made a killing on the day.

I sold eight books, which is one per hour. Perhaps that sounds miserable, but I keep telling myself it's name recognition, not dollars, that I'm chasing. Isn't that how it works? How else can I expect my 'fame' to spread?

Oh, if I'd been selling top hats rather than books, I'd have been laughing all the way to the bank. Paul, if you're reading this, please take a bow.

29 September 2022

Philosopher Farmer

Jabiru who knows where its next meal is coming from

A jabiru is a lovely (and highly intelligent) bird found in Northern Australia. An adult bird stands at least a metre tall.

I snapped this one some years ago at Kakadu National Park in the Top End of the Northern Territory, a place where they thrive. Then, on my recent road trip out west in Queensland, I came across another of these adorable birds on a property where we stayed for three days. Actually, at the time, I was quite surprised. I hadn't thought jabirus ventured that far south.

The property was more or less due west of where we live on the coast near Rockhampton, at a quite hefty distance from the sea, very remote, and of prodigious size as befits an Australian outback property. Dan (not his real name) ran it. He had nursed the injured bird to health, and now, though preferring to go its own way, the critter always liked to stay within cooee of the homestead.

I had first talked to Dan on the phone, when organizing the farm stay. His Aussie accent was so thick you would need a blade of the keenest obsidium to cut through it. I thought to myself, What *am* I letting myself in for here? Who *is* this bogan? I needn't have worried. When I got to meet him in the flesh, we (both of us, I believe) really clicked. It's extremely rare that I hit things off with a person to the extent I did with Dan.

Janet and I were accommodated for the duration of our stay in a converted shearing shed. When I say 'converted', believe me it was luxurious. Janet, who never says no to a little luxury, *was* impressed.

I judged Dan to be in his early forties, with a wife (whom I shall call Adele) somewhat younger, and a girl child about six months old. These three people were the only permanent residents of the property, which must have made for a very lonely existence. Mostly, the only company they had, apart from paying visitors like me, were themselves and the contractors brought in as required for specialist jobs, e.g. mustering by helicopter. More on this later.

During our stay, I talked to Dan quite a bit. He was sent by his farming family to Rockhampton Grammar School, but didn't last there long. A regimented life with academic overtones did not suit him at all. He ducked classes and was soon 'let go' by the school. Accordingly, he *went*, and bummed around in the far north of the country, before settling down to run the family farm. He was self educated, and very effectively at that. He was no ignoramus. Nor was he a fool.

Sensing, I guess, that I was not the usual punter to whom he might throw open his farm, he wanted to know my back-story in detail. So I gave him the goods, from my early childhood on. On learning of my background in nuclear physics – a background surely as rare, in Australia, as alchemy – he asked if I thought nuclear energy was a go-er for Australia, given that contemporary reactors were reportedly a lot safer that those of previous generations. I replied that I suspected these selfsame safety features did not come free, but would require customers to fork out a hefty premium, putting the finished product out of economic consideration in comparison with alternative energy sources, e.g. renewables.

This, then, was how that imposing edifice comprising Dan's self education was built. Brick by brick as required and with the help of his irrepressible spirit of inquiry. I had provided him with the latest brick.

Dan showed me round the property. He ran mainly cattle and dorpers, the latter being a breed of sheep farmed for its meat rather than for its wool. I was impressed to find that he ran the property on sound sustainability principles verging on the scientific. He was no redneck farmer.

For example, he was in the process of reclaiming, over the long term, a large swathe of unproductive land, by ploughing a tight series of ditches across it at right angles to the direction of water flow across it. Thereby, water run-off after rain was slowed right down to something approaching a trickle. He pointed out to me two adjacent fields, one of which he had treated in this way and the other which he had not. After what had been only a couple of years, the field that had been given the treatment looked distinctly promising, whereas the other looked rubbish.

Naturally, Dan was all in favour of capping renegade bores that accessed the Great Artesian Basin, either with permanent plugs or with on/off valves. On his very own property, he participated willingly and eagerly in the project to give the Basin a chance to replenish by this means. That this simple and obvious tactic is starting to bear fruit is readily verified by a certain recent and remarkable event that happened on his property.

So, let me fill you in.

On the occasion, an agitated visitor to the property told him a camel was stuck in the mud 'out there'. There's no mud out there, said Dan. But he followed the visitor to the location and, sure enough, there was a camel up to its neck in a mud pool that had never existed before, not in *his* tenure over the land anyway. This was a clear example of the Great Artesian Basin breaking through the surface as a result of its natural recharge. Nature was just putting things right again after a century or so of abuse.

They pulled the unfortunate animal out, of course. Then they marvelled at what they saw. I marvelled too at what Dan was showing me now, and which I would describe as a rejuvinated 'mound spring' of the type the first nations' people are/were so glad to have at their disposal around the Oodnadatta Track and elsewhere.

This was science in action. Those inclined to religion might see the finger of God pointing. 'And here by My grace ye shall have a fresh water spring.'

Dan also knew his local history. He showed me a plant called nardoo that grew as a weed in parts of his property. Nardoo was/is used by traditional aborigines as a food source. Its seeds could be ground into a powder which could then be used as a type of flour. It was also used as food by the explorers Burke and Wills in their (literal) dying days.

The trouble is that, unless nardoo is processed in a particular way (which the aborigines have always known about, of course), it would do more harm than good. Without appropriate processing, it prevented the body from absorbing vitamin B. The aborigines may or may not have heard about vitamin B, but they sure as hell knew/know how to process nardoo.

It was because Burke and Wills *didn't* know this vital information (they ate the stuff raw) that nardoo contributed to the bad (and preventable) end to which they famously came.

The most exciting time for me happened the next day.

The dorper ewes needed to be mustered. They were – almost to the last animal – heavily pregnant, and about to drop their load. At present, they were grazing in an open paddock which afforded them no cover should birds of prey choose to swoop on the new born lambs. Which they, avian intelligent and opportunistic, would certainly be inclined to do.

So, the ewes were to be herded into a heavily treed and adjacent paddock. I was to observe the whole procedure as it unfolded. Adele would drive me to the location in their sturdy 4WD.

The helicopter was already in the air as we arrived. Dan was below on his industrial-strength bike, giving ground support. The terrain he had to cover was rough, presenting (I imagined) a not insignificant threat to the integrity of his ankles and other susceptible parts.

To watch several hundred (perhaps even in excess of a thousand) pregnant ewes being funnelled through a narrow gate into the wooded paddock, their heavy backsides bobbing in the breeze, was a sight I shall not forget. It was all over in about thirty minutes, thanks to the chopper pilot. Mission accomplished. Dan told me that, without aerial support it would have taken the best part of a day.

Job over, Dan suggested we go fishing. A handy creek passed through his property close to the homestead and, given it was a *la nina* year, the water in it was up. That's where we headed. When Dan had identified a suitable site on this watercourse, we set to our task.

Let me make it clear. I am not a fisher. I don't know the ropes at all. So Dan had to bait and cast my line for me. I imagined him thinking, Who is this turkey? But (smiling to himself, I fancy) he was the epitome of patience and tolerance. Amused? Yes. But he derived pleasure in some small way from my inept company.

And we had *other* company. A kibitzer. The jabiru.

I got the first catch. A turtle, for Pete's sake. Then Dan pulled in two plump yellowtails, one of which he fed to the jabiru. He threw back the other, as he did the turtle.

Afterwards, the sun low, and we sucking on beers, I asked Dan how he got to learn all he needed to know about farm management, particularly the forward-thinking stuff apropos sustainable practices. Forgive me if I paraphrase his answer. I'm afraid I forget his exact words. But the gist of his reply was, I listen to the old guys.

What he meant was (and of this I am certain): if they've been on the land all that time and they're still making a crust, they must know what works and what doesn't. It's that simple. Talk to the old guys.

I'll tell you someone who knows what works and what doesn't. B'Jesus. It's got to be Dan. After all, he has figured whose are the right brains to pick.

In the title to this blog, I've described Dan as a 'philosopher farmer'. I believe that description is appropriate. A philosopher is someone with a thirst for inquiry, someone whose tools of trade are the questions, 'why' and 'how'. The ancient philosophers, Greek of course, built their city states using these tools.

We're not talking city states here. We're talking sheep-stations.

My Life Presumed Post-COVID

13 October 2022

Kon'nichiwa Japan

According to reports, Japan will be open to foreign tourism *sans* restrictions come the middle of this month. Since Covid presented itself uninvited to the world, all sorts of onerous conditions for visits to Japan had been put in place and kept there assiduously, to the extent that the country was effectively off-limits as a tourist destination. Especially to people like me, who like to organize all their travel independently of guides, travel agents, and bureaucracy in general.

But now, official sources tell me that all this is out the window as of 11 October 22. A red-letter day for the likes of me.

I love Japan. It is my favorite country bar none to explore. Not even my own country, Australia, can measure up for this purpose, though it might come in a distant second. The people of Oz are great to deal with even if their sardonic take on life can grate at times. And there are some wonderful things to see in Oz, especially the blood red massif of Uluru rising out of a dead flat plain, in my opinion the most thrilling sight in the world. And the palette from which the colours of the Australian landscape are drawn is like no other I have ever encountered. Where else can you see a blue like that of an Australian sky?

But, regrettably, Australia falls down badly when it comes to cuisine. Outside of the major cities, the food is quite disappointing, with a couple of notable exceptions such as the fresh barramundi to be found in the Gulf region. Not so in Japan, where the cuisine everywhere – food *and* drink – is in my opinion unmatched in the world.

And the people are so very friendly. Take the photo above, snapped by me in a modest little restaurant in Nagasaki in 2019. That is the proprietor you see, welcoming us. Look at the way her whole face lights up. That is no stitched-on smile such as celebrities or spruikers might flash when on the make. That is the real deal. And I have many other photos of people like this – from Tokyo, Osaka, Fukuoka, etc. – all of them with a smile so genuine it makes McCoy look like an outrageous pretender.

I should tell the story of how we found this restaurant. It was about 5 p.m. when Janet and I were reconnoitering for possible eating places for that evening. It was closed of course, but we thought we might pull back the curtain a tad and take a surreptitious peek inside. As we did so, Janet tripped on the step and fell flat on her face. She literally fell into the restaurant.

That's when the lovely young lady above came quickly on the scene. She fussed over Janet, ready to give her first aid on the spot, except that Janet was (mercifully) uninjured. She was profusely apologetic, even though we and our unwarranted timidity were fully to blame. She helped Janet to her feet, and we went away. But we came back for dinner that evening. And every subsequent evening while we were in Nagasaki.

Needless to say the food, the sake, the service, and the company were everything we could have hoped for and more.

My very first visit to Japan had been several decades earlier, in the 1970s, when the Company I then worked for as a young research scientist sent me to Tokyo to attend a couple of technical conferences. I was completely taken aback when my application to the Company had been accepted and, even though back then Japan was not my preferred overseas destination, I grabbed the opportunity with open arms.

From the moment I touched down, Japan seemed like a thoroughly alien place. Putting my misgivings aside, I checked into my plush hotel, and registered for the conferences. From the very start of proceedings, it became obvious to me that the participants, mostly male and American, were from the dyed-in-the-wool publish-or-perish brigade. None of what they presented had any application to the research I was doing back home, and perhaps not elsewhere. I was bored. Worse still, lunch was a deadly affair where participants sat around long tables and spent their time desperately trying to 'network'. This was LinkedIn with a flesh-and-blood face, and on steroids. I decided quite early on that this scene was not for me. From the very first day, I attended only enough of the sessions to placate my conscience, i.e. to make me feel I was doing the right thing by the Company and its shareholders, who were, after all, paying my way.

I hit the streets of Tokyo, according to my preconceptions an alien place. It turned out to be a cornucopia of wonders. Amazing department stores, much bigger than anything back home, whose purpose seemed to be to delight and entertain its customers while it took their money. Half a dozen plump peaches, gift wrapped with bright ribbons and all the rest of the knobs, at the point of sale. A Metro system that whisked you near-instantaneously to the other side of the city, to the bright lights of Shinjuku for example. Spectacular and drama-filled dance routines, enough to thrill to the back teeth any innocent abroad that, as I was to realize decades later, were probably based on the famed *awa-odori* tradition of the city of Tokushima. The ubiquitous vending machines, almost as numerous as people, making me wonder perhaps if Japan had invented them. And the frighteningly life-like plastic models of weird-looking foods on display in the windows of eating houses. And, of course, the bullet trains.

I took one of these trains when I decided to spend a weekend in Kyoto. I stayed there in lavish accommodation at the Company's expense. Without feeling any guilt now, I booked a room that had its very own private Japanese garden.

I also took day trips to Hakone and Nikko. All the people I met were genuinely delighted to see me, as per the lady from Nagasaki in the photo. I found to my amazement that it was impossible to get lost or stranded in Japan. Wait a tad and some form of transport would appear like magic, in timely fashion, and on time, to take you to your destination. Was this a dream?

There was one fly in the ointment: the food. It looked so utterly strange. Sushi was totally unfamiliar in Oz back then. All that raw fish seemed to me about as appetizing as a shit sandwich. So, how did I handle the situation? I did what any sensible person would do. For the first two or three days, I ate nothing but ice-cream.

There comes a point where such a diet, no matter how good the ice-cream, will leave you feeling desperately famished. I had a problem. Finally, driven by a gnawing emptiness of the gut, I braved a restaurant in Tokyo around lunch time. At a neighbouring table, I noticed a *gaijin*, probably American, eating something that didn't look too raw. I asked the waiter for the same.

To say it hit the spot would be an understatement. It hit so many spots all at once that spots all over the shop would have been ducking for cover. I asked my neighbour what I had been eating. He replied, *unagi*, going on to explain that this was smoked eel on a bed of rice.

It was delicious.

Unsurprisingly, I ate lots of *unagi* from this point on. Then, one day, feeling unaccountably emboldened, I entered a restaurant that, judging by its window displays, specialized in raw fish. I sat at the bar with Japanese people all around me, and ordered *miso* soup followed by *sashimi*, washed down with Kirin beer.

This was assuredly one of the greatest meals of my life. Not just because it satisfied the taste test, but because it represented my initiation into what is arguable the world's greatest cuisine. Tokyo was no longer an alien place. I had embraced it, and it had embraced me.

Let's return to the present day. In fact, let's anticipate 11 October 22. As I write this, I realize that was only two days prior. You'll be reading this post *after* this crucial date had passed. This is the date, as I mentioned, when truly independent travel to Japan shall become available to all those desiring it.

So why haven't we bought plane tickets?

We'll bide our time. Let the dust settle. Let others more rash test the waters. Let the airlines sort out their myriad problems.

We'll *choose* our time. Our excuse is we want to see the autumn colours, starting in Hokkaido and wending our way south. So we plan to make the trip starting in October 2023.

Kon'nichiwa Japan.

3 November 2022

Pain

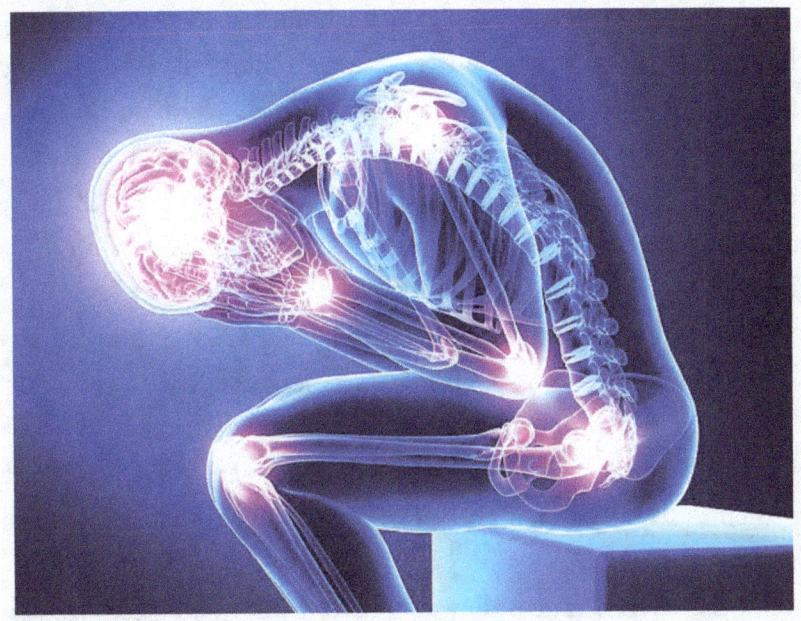

When I was a child, I was told that pain was nature's way of telling me something was wrong, and that it needed my attention. Great idea, I thought. So all I had to do was tell nature I had received her message loud and clear and then, perhaps in tandem with my parents or doctor, go about setting the problem right.

Oh, no. It doesn't work that way. Nature has her own rules and, bloody minded as she is, persists in repeating the message, over and over, over and over, with doomsday seemingly the only release for the recipient. This is what we know as chronic pain. We've all had it, and will have it again.

I have it now.

All the muscles in my neck and legs ache excruciatingly. I hobble rather than walk, on leg muscles that feel battered and bruised, always pushing through a pain barrier when doing so. Often, I have headaches typical of a bout of flu. Accompanying these headaches is what I call brain fog. At moments when the fog disperses slightly, I am able to add a few more words to this blog. My reading program, always a pleasure to me, has stalled. At this time of year, it might have included some Shakespeare, but at the moment I feel I'd be hard pressed to cope with *Thomas the Tank Engine*.

This has been going on now for the best part of a month.

Janet, my life partner, has given me unquestioned support during this time, for which I am immensely grateful. This is the sickest I have been in my adult life. She has served up meals and medicines to me on demand, even when I make that 'demand' at impossible times like 3 a.m. I know it is taking its toll on her but, under the circumstances, I'm unable to think of a better strategy. Except perhaps to get well. That would indeed be a blessing for both of us.

What has the medical profession got to say? Well, let's make one thing clear at the outset. Nobody suspects Covid. I have had countless RAT tests, and one very recent PCR test. They all came up negative.

My doctor, Richard Shepherd, whom I respect, doesn't yet know what's wrong with me, but has had me through (and *is having* me through) a battery of tests, in an apparent attempt to find out what the hell it is I've got. At one stage, he uttered the phrase 'para flu', but I suspect that's the type of answer doctors trot out to their patients when they don't really have an answer.

The last test, done on a blood sample, revealed that the degree of severity of my muscle inflammation was one hundred percent. Holey doolly. Isn't that the top of the range? I don't believe Richard ever thought I was a malingerer, but this surely puts the issue beyond any reasonable doubt.

Since then, I have had another blood test, this one to find out if have any of the markers for Ross River Fever, Q fever, Barmah Forest Fever, Dengue Fever, or any of the other beasties in the stable of this diabolical family. I await the results.

Night time is interesting.

Since, by all reports, my inflamed muscles lie just below the skin, I find it difficult to find a comfortable position in which to sleep. So, I mostly toss and turn. When I *do* drop off, usually in the wee hours, I often have dreams that are – let's just say – beyond weird.

For your potential interest, I relate one of these dreams here.

Imagine a huge single-story villa spread over several hectares, consisting of countless interlocking square rooms, each unfurnished, and measuring about 4m by 4m. Each of the rooms has four doors, one in each of its walls. I am there because I've heard there is a musical event going on here someplace. As I go from room to room, I am unable to find said musical event. I imagine I hear its strains wafting to me from a distance. It is *The Four Seasons* by Antonio Vivaldi,

What I *do* find in each room is a prominent right-wing figure of some note holding forth to a nut-job audience in the single digits. Some of those holding forth are local, some international. The crew from Sky News After Dark is well represented in the premises. So, in the first room, I find that grinning idiot, Rowan Dean, who seems to believe that his inane visage is some sort of asset to his persona or perhaps to the incoherent cause he is trying to espouse. I exit hurriedly.

The next room contains Richard Bolt, complete with his phoney gravitas. He has a way of starting from unfounded premises, then expanding upon them with impeccable logic, to reach (unsurprisingly) quite outrageous conclusions. I suspect he picked up this technique from Bob Santamaria, a pundit some of you may remember from decades back, but Bob did it with much better style than this upstart Bolt ever did. I exit hurriedly.

In the next room is that long-legged woman whose name I can never recall. And indeed why should I? To steal a line from Gareth Evans, it saves time. Her potted populist opinions are an insult to intelligence. I exit hurriedly.

The next room contains – I kid you not – a cameo appearance from beyond the grave. Werner von Braun, no less. Not wanting to hear some ideological spiel on rocket science, with an emphasis possibly on its effective use against the *untermenschen*, from a ghost no less, and delivered with a Kraut accent, I exit hurriedly.

I fully expect to find Adolf Hitler next, but instead I get Vladimir Putin. A fair swap, some would argue. With a perfunctory wave to my old mate and a few encouraging words ('keep up the good work, Vlad') I make my exit.

So, on to Nigel Farage, with a mouth big enough to take the head of a mop. Had one been on hand, I think I might have obliged.

… and so on and so on …

So, as if my personal pain wasn't boring enough in itself, I had to be subjected to these unfunny clowns taking up my precious moments of fitful sleep,

You, my ever-so-precious readers, must now understand that,

for the time being anyway, I may not be able to pump out these blogs at the same rate as I have been, which I believe is one every two or three weeks. You might have some understanding of how difficult it has been to get *this one* out. So, please give me a break while I sort this shit out, this shit that has beset me without mercy.

    I expect to be back. Just not soon.

1 December 2022

… Till the Fat Lady Sings

Regrettably, the fat lady is *not* yet ready to sing for me. Having suffered, without warning or pity, a massive surge of inflammation in the major muscles of my body, a surge the medical profession can't explain, I am now in a sort of remission enabling me to function to a significant degree. I'm not bedridden any more, I can walk and drive, and the terrible brain fog I've been enduring is becoming less and less frequent.

I've found that the medical profession takes this type of event quite seriously. It can be alleviated almost overnight using a massive dose of a steroid known as prednisolone. That's the stuff they prescribed for me. The problem is it's not easy to come down from such a massive dose of steroids. Serious withdrawal symptoms lurk just round the corner and, quite rightly, medicos like to monitor the process they call 'tapering', which means lowering the dose slowly and carefully while organizing regular blood tests to see that the inflammation really has disappeared.

That's the point I am at as of now. The treatment may not be worse than the ailment itself, but it certainly isn't benign. I am in the second stage of a two-stage recovery.

But nobody listens to a whinger, so let's change the subject.

Back in the dark ages, in the second half of the 20th century, I was a green young pup living for an extended period in London. Naturally, I found it imperative to visit English pubs. At one of those that I frequented, I met and befriended a young Japanese man of about my age, whom I shall call Hideki. That's not his real name. I'm not sure I ever knew his real name. So, as a name, Hideki will serve the purpose. To me, Hideki – despite his limited English – was a useful and engaging drinking partner for a time, and I was glad to have him in my orbit.

I never found out how Hideki made his living in London, but always assumed he played a junior role in either journalism or the diplomatic service.

This pub was Hideki's regular haunt every evening, when he could always be found sitting on a pint by himself in a secluded corner. It was not my regular haunt, but when I paid it a visit, I always sought out Hideki.

What we had in common was we both harked from distant shores on the other side of the world. But Hideki was feeling homesick to a greater degree than I. The distance he felt could not be measured purely in kilometres. He missed the comfort of his familiar Japanese culture.

But, in competition with this negative feeling, he felt an overwhelming fascination with the foreign culture he now felt himself immersed in. I heard the excitement in his upwardly-inflected verbal language and saw it in his restive body language. His eyes would dart around the room in which we sat, taking everything in, as if he were witnessing a strange new ritual never seen at home. This was nothing like the *izakaya* he frequented back in Tokyo.

The characters who crowded the bar were rough, and treated the middle-aged barmaid to a persistent stream of ribald derision. Her response to this was total disdain. This would *never* have happened in Hideki's *izakaya* back home. No siree.

More of the woman who pulled the beers later.

The room in which we sat? Maybe you can, or maybe you can't, conjure up a picture of a typical London pub – an essential watering hole its clients called 'the local' – an example of which seemed to be on the corner of every little backstreet in Inner London. It usually had an absurd name, like *Toad and Hole*, of obscure origin, perhaps harking back centuries.

Inside, it was the very definition of cosy. Having secured your pint of best bitter from the crowded bar, you could retire to one of many nooks available for the purpose, to sip your beverage, and engage in intimate and civilized conversation under its benevolent influence. The furniture we sat in, and all the trimmings round the room were of a dark wood – walnut perhaps – that was ever so easy on the eye. By day, the lighting was the weak London sunshine that was the deal in this part of the world and, by night, it was a soft and warm artificial concoction barely able to penetrate to the nook we sat in.

Yes, cosiness was assuredly the order of the day (or night) in this neck of the woods.

Not so cosy, perhaps, was the woman I mentioned behind the

bar pulling beers. You would not want to meddle with this woman. I imagined that, instead of cereal for breakfast, she would eat a bowl of two-inch flat-head nails.

The aspect of the Anglo-Saxon pub rites that fascinated Hideki more than any other was closing time which, from memory, was 10 p.m. At five minutes to this hour, the woman at the bar would announce sternly, 'Last drinks, gentlemen', regardless of whether or not there were any female drinkers present, or whether 'gentleman' was an apt descriptor for any of those of the male gender that crowded the region of the bar. This would send a shiver of pleasure mixed with terror through Hideki's body. He had been waiting for this moment, and the sheer thrill of it was evident in his features.

That woman is very terrible, Hideki would say as a shudder of fear and delight rippled across his face.

We have a saying in English, I said, that goes 'It's not over till the fat lady sings.'

Does she sing too? asked Hideki. That would be very *very* terrible.

I don't believe she actually sings, I said. And she's not fat.

Hideki seemed a little disappointed, but nothing would dampen his vicarious anticipation of what might happen in the next five minutes.

At precisely 10 p.m. the woman placed her hands flat on the bar, leaned forward, and announced with an authority not to be brooked, Closing time, gentlemen.

Hideki was excited beyond all reasonable bounds.

That women is very terrible, he said.

I responded to her edict by leaving the bar, hanging around in the lane-way outside waiting for Hideki to emerge. He was staying around for the crunch, obviously determined to see how terrible this woman could really get.

He emerged, bright-eyed. He was like a schoolboy in thrall of a spanking by his school-ma'am. I'll never know the circumstances of his final encounter with the woman, but I'm sure he would have behaved throughout with the impeccable politeness characteristic of Japanese people.

Terrible, he said. That woman is very terrible.

We went our separate ways. I imagined Hideki turning up tomorrow night and each night after that for further encounters with the very terrible woman, a sequence of encounters that brings to mind Nietzsche's eternal returns. For Hideki, the (not so) fat lady never ever did sing.

I'm hoping, late in 2022, on my bed of pain, the fat lady shall deign to sing for me.

15 December 2022

Good Will Towards Men

Even as a humanist/atheist, I can still condone the sentiment expressed in the above title, which comes from St Luke's gospel in the Christian bible. Except to say that in the 21st century, its scope should be expanded so as not (apparently) to rule out women.

I am always moved when I see an expression of this precept. The above picture is an example. It was sent to me recently by my granddaughter, Beth, who is in her late teens, and whose mother, my daughter, has sadly chosen to remain estranged from me for most of her adult life. The inscribed bauble hangs on the family Christmas tree thousands of kilometres from me on the other side of the continent. I am, of course, the 'grandad' referred to in the inscription. The date (2014) shows the first year in which the bauble was hung. Presumably, it has been hung every year since then, side by side with baubles for other members of the extended family.

I am touched. Thank you, Beth, for the good will you show. You are a sweet girl.

Similar good will is on display in Catholic churches at midnight Mass on Christmas Eve. If, like me, you are a non-believer, you can ignore the religious overtones, and treat it as a secular message. Precisely at midnight, you are urged to shake hands with or embrace those on either side of you in the pew. When I first encountered this practice, dragged to church by my then girlfriend, a Catholic, I was taken completely by surprise. The person next to me, whom I didn't know from Adam, turned to me and extended his hand. For a few anxious seconds, I didn't know how to respond, then the penny dropped.

Once again, I was touched by this simple display of good will.

Christmas is not my favorite time of year. I am always glad when it, and New Year, are over, and life has a chance to return to normal. In the run-up to Christmas, the manic juggernaut known as 'advertising', creation of a rampant commercial sector, switches into overdrive. Most of this advertising consists of iterations on the big con. Con bordering on scam. Most of what it peddles is blatant misinformation, designed to dupe the most vulnerable in our community into lining the pockets of capitalist enterprises by parting with their hard-earned without any proportionate reward.

And what might these latter-day snake oil sales people think about good will towards men?

Are you serious? Get real. Where's the profit to be had in that?

Capitalist enterprise has seriously gone off the rails. Instead of looking at the essential message of Christmas, which message I believe can be taken either as religious or as secular, it has chosen to weaponize Christmas to its own venal advantage.

I suggest to you that it may be instructive to look at the text in full, i.e. go back to St Luke. There you'll find written 'on earth peace, and goodwill toward men.'

Peace on earth?

In which incarnation would that be?

19 January 2023

Big Pharma: the Least Worst Alternative

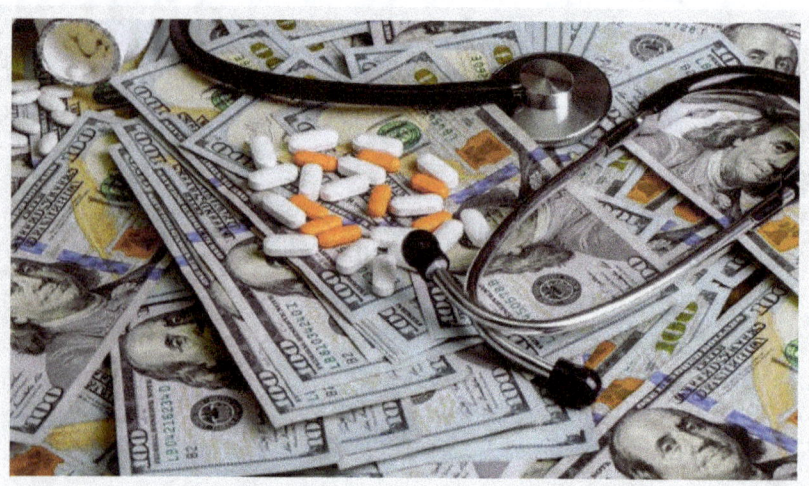

When you are in a painful medical state like mine (finally identified by the profession as *polymyalgia rheumatica* or PMR), it would be a mistake not to go with what is proven to work by solid scientific evidence. There's no reason to be shy about that phrase 'scientific evidence'. It's really just an extension of what we as a species can confirm with our own senses.

And I'm sorry to say here that what works is big bad pharma. They have all the evidence. Despite the profit-driven abuses we all know of in the industry and despite all the side effects and contra-indications of their products, these products have been put through a rigorous evidence-gathering procedure to establish their effectiveness, for the most part, under appropriate medical supervision.

It's the best we've got so we should grit our teeth and learn to love it. Would you in your right mind, or even in your wrong mind for that matter, go with alternative 'medicine', for which there is little or no evidence base? Would you go with the siren calls of all the self-appointed gurus who would like you to believe based on hearsay that X or Y (or bleach perhaps?) is the magic cure for your ailments?

I am taking so many pills at the moment that I believe I would rattle if shaken. They are all evidence based. I wouldn't waste my money or risk my health on alternatives.

Agreed, I'm not even sure as I write this that it's me doing the writing. I write through a fog induced by a pain-killing prescription drug called *palexia*. Bad as it makes my head feel, it works, and buys me time while the medical profession figure out how to treat the underlying condition with yet more prescriptions drugs. Which they will in due course. The *palexia* also gives me the breathing space enabling me to get on with a bit of physiotherapy in deference to my wasted muscles.

But the final cure, at which point the beast PMR is eradicated from my body for good, may take months.

So, please regard the flow of my blogs (following this one) as being in abeyance for the moment. It's a temporary but necessary pause. The spirit is ready, but my mind and body are not up to it right now. Give me time, and I'll be back. I'm not retiring.

Stay tuned. This is not my swansong. And stay away from the snake oil.

30 March 2023

Nuclear Waste Disposal in Oz: a Can to Be Kicked Down the Road

Nuclear waste is a problem for Australia right now but, in future decades, it is likely to become a much more significant problem for us, particularly if the much spruiked nuclear-powered submarine program – known by the clunky acronym AUKUS – manages to get off the ground.

I'm worried about AUKUS for multiple reasons. The economic implications are huge for us, particularly the tab we'll have to pick up: on present counts, in excess of a third of a trillion dollars. Geoffrey Robertson, the high-profile human rights barrister, has noted that the cost of defence procurements of this nature typically blows out to something like three times the original estimate. On this basis, we could actually be up for in excess of a trillion. Our government likes to point out that, when spread out over 30 or so successive budgets, the cost is not so very prohibitive. But 368 billion dollars overall – that's the present oft-quoted figure before any consideration of blow-outs – would buy a shitload of useful things. One I can think of is a brand new national electricity grid, capable of handling the requirements of the renewable energy future to which, as I understand, we are committed. I'm sure you can think of others.

Then there are the geopolitical implications. China's rapid development over the last few decades – economically, technically, and strategically – is plain for all to see, and they just love to flaunt it, sometimes in a very confronting way. Jealous of China's increasing assertiveness, the US is more than a little inclined to push back. But this is the US's battle, not ours. We don't have to go along with such antics.

Since WW2, we have sheltered militarily and otherwise under the umbrella we assume the US is holding out for us. But the world has changed. It may no longer be prudent for us to take this approach. The umbrella appears increasingly leaky. Perhaps we should look more closely now to the countries of the western Pacific, including China, when addressing our security concerns. Needless to say, we would have to keep our eyes wide open, a given in any foreign policy consideration. Such a change of policy – to regional co-operation rather than regional confrontation – would sit uncomfortably with AUKUS. And on more counts than one.

But I want to deal with an implication of a quite different nature, and no less serious, that AUKUS has in store for us. Assuming these nuclear powered subs get up and running, are we equipped to handle the new technology their acquisition would require?

I am a rarity in Australia. I have a Ph.D. in nuclear physics. So, I consider myself pretty well qualified to express opinions on matters nuclear. I like to think that, when it comes to the sort of technology to which AUKUS will require we commit, my voice is a little more informed than that of your average Joe.

We in Oz will be going from babes-in-the-wood as regards nuclear matters to the recipients of state-of-the-art nuclear technology, involving highly enriched uranium fuel, i.e. the stuff capable of being used to make nuclear weapons. We'll have to get ready for this in a tearing great hurry, and Murphy's law says that, in our unseemly haste, things will go wrong. Given the magnitude of our inexperience and the complexity of the technology, it will likely be *multiple* things that go wrong, and they will go *badly* wrong. It's naive to expect any other outcome.

We have no skin in the game. The only phase of the nuclear fuel cycle for which we have (or have had) the physical infrastructure properly in place is the mining of uranium ore. We have (wisely, I believe) declined to be involved in the other phases, e.g. energy production via nuclear power plants. Because of this, we have had no opportunity to 'learn the trade'. Nor do we have the educational infrastructure needed to train personnel, such as nuclear engineers and the like. Where is there a Homer Simpson to be found in Australia?

We are in trouble. Big trouble. We're about to be thrown in the deep end before we've had swimming lessons.

In this blog, I'd like to consider (as just one example of a much more general problem) what hopefully is the final phase of the nuclear fuel cycle: the disposal of nuclear waste. A moment of truth for us, and for our political masters, must surely have come when it dawned on us (and on them) that we, the denizens of Oz, would be required, as part of the AUKUS arrangements, to deal with the waste from the reactors driving the submarines. That's we in AU, not those in the UK or in the US. It's *we* who'll be left holding the proverbial can.

But given the projected design of the subs – with the reactors supposedly not needing any attention until the subs are decommissioned – isn't it a fact that we won't face this problem until the useful life of the subs and their reactors has ended? Only then will the hard shells containing the reactors be cracked open. Only then will the fuel rods – bristling with fission products, highly enriched uranium residue, and by-product plutonium – get to see the light of day.

Some would urge us to keep things in perspective. Apropos of the above considerations, wouldn't we have thirty or so years of grace after we take delivery of the spanking new subs before we have to deal with the problem of waste disposal? Let's get real here, some would say. Most of us will be dead and buried by then.

This is a way of thinking to which we (sadly) are fast becoming inured. Let's give the can a hefty kick down the road. Isn't it yet another of the problems we can bequeath to our children and grandchildren? They come from sturdy stock. They'll be up to the task. Just like they'll take the effects of global heating in their stride when the time comes, while we, their forebears in the here and now, are free to burn up those fossil fuels with preposterous impunity. We all know that Greta Thunberg is mentally deranged. Andrew Bolt told us so.

Getting back to nuclear waste disposal …

Have we the ability to dispose of this waste? Well, we run

a small nuclear reactor for the purposes of research, and the supply of the needs of nuclear medicine, at Lucas Heights, on the outskirts of Sydney. And, for decades now, we have not been able to find an acceptable depository for the waste even from this piddling operation. The nimbys, mostly well-off white Anglos, are ready to squash with vigor any suggestion it should be in their backyard. Likewise, the first nations' people, once bitten twice shy over Maralinga and the like, are ready to resist vehemently any attempt to have it put on their land.

The AUKUS reactors will produce a new category of waste, known as HLW (or 'high-level nuclear waste') with which we have hitherto not been required to deal. Inexplicably, none of the waste from Lucas Heights has been classified as high-level. HLW, essentially comprising spent fuel rods, presents the most problems when the time comes for disposal. These rods contain a highly radioactive mix of enriched uranium residue, serendipitous plutonium, and fission products. These are Frankenstein substances not existing in nature. They are inimical to life on our planet.

Such waste would probably be exported initially to one of the handful of countries around the world that run nuclear reprocessing plants. France comes to mind. Once there, commercially useful uranium and plutonium would be extracted by them, and gladly accepted for their own reactor program, before the remaining waste, bristling with really nasty fission products of no dollar value, would be returned to us, possibly in vitrified form, i.e. as very heavy glass-like bricks. These bricks, our problem now, would represent for us a management problem on a scale with which we have not previously had to cope. Because of their high temperature, a consequence of the internal heat generated through their ongoing radioactive decay, we would have to store these bricks underwater for a considerable time, measured in years, until they cooled down sufficiently. But where? Then once they *are* cool enough, we would have to find a suitably stable geological structure, deep underground, in which they could be stored safely for hundreds of years. But where?

Do we really want to expose ourselves to this level of difficulty and hazard? If AUKUS manages to get itself up, we surely will have to.

What the hell *are* we letting ourselves in for?

13 April 2023

Small Miracles

A life well lived should consist of a series of small miracles. I'm not the only person who has said this, or something along similar lines. But, in times of hardship, which is the here and now for many people, it begs to be said again. I don't want to belittle the real hardships many people are enduring, and for which I suspect unfortunately there are no silver bullets, but what I have to say here about small miracles may, in some inscrutable way, help them to bear these hardships, and so gather the strength to see their way through to better times beyond them.

Consider the above photo taken on my mobile phone – please

excuse the indifferent quality – of one example of a small miracle. That's my hand lurking behind it, so you can see how small the miracle actually is. In the front of my house, I have two trees – mother and daughter – that bear dozens, perhaps hundreds, of these beautiful pink frilly trumpets. If you asked me to identify the trees, I would not be able to. I am no botanist, not even a keen gardener, just an aficionado of small miracles.

At times, these trees shed these astonishing pink flowers all over my lawn and driveway, so that their totality resembles a pink carpet. It is as if the trees themselves are sending me pink kisses to thank me for planting them and allowing them space in which to thrive. And thrive they do. 'Mother' is about six metres tall, and 'daughter' is fast catching up.

I experience a tiny thrill, from the top of my head to the tip of my toes, and from the surface of my skin to the inner marrow of my bones, every time I lay eyes upon this small miracle of the pink trumpets.

Another small miracle I often see on my turf, is the ladybird, a common variety of beetle, with which you would all be familiar. It is like a tiny polished jewel, albeit spotted with what some may call imperfections. A *living* jewel. It is as beautiful as a ruby, though perhaps not as much valued as a ruby by us humans. Perhaps we need to rethink our values.

When the ladybird senses she (or mayhap he?) is receiving too much attention from human admirers, her hemispherical shell will split down the middle, the two flaps so formed opening up to reveal yet another small wonder: the finest of fine wings. The criterion of fineness often invoked in such a context as this is 'paper thin'. But the finest paper I know would seem like a chunky and unbending plank compared with the fineness and flexibility of ladybird wings.

And so off she flies.

> *Ladybird, ladybird*
> *fly away home.*
> *Your house is on fire.*
> *Your children shall burn.*

Oh, dear. Such an outcome, as expressed in this ditty, would indubitably put a dampener on my small miracle, so I trust anything as dire as this grim take on matters would not happen on my watch. Stay safe, ladybird, and that goes for your precious children as well.

Small miracles are not always visual. Any one of the senses may become the conduit for a small miracle, including the sense of hearing.

On one recent still summer's night, I woke for no particular reason at 3 a.m., that hour even the most dedicated insomniac will generally sleep through, and took myself out onto my back verandah. Leaning on the railing, I looked west out over the streets of the small village in which I live. I saw no people. I saw no stray dogs. I saw no vehicles. I saw no crocodiles. I saw no zombies. I saw no vampires. I saw only houses, whose occupants gave every appearance of having been detained in the land of Nod, and myriad botanical varieties whose leaves could find no breeze to stir them from deepest lethargy.

But, in this case, the small miracle wasn't what I saw or didn't see. It was the silence. The absence of any aural effect was in my face. I swear the complete lack of sound screamed at me.

This scream of silence would never be heard in a big city, whose residents I could only pity at that special moment for me. It was a manifestation delivered benevolently by the absence of sound, as it soothes ever so gently the network of neurons that constitutes the brain. It was the aural equivalent of nothing. Nothing. No thing. Zilch. And there can be no smaller miracle than zilch, by definition the very smallest of small miracles, bringing in its wake momentary and blissful peace to frazzled humans.

The small miracle of silence.

And, as I stood there, yet another small miracle came into my mind, not one I actually saw at this moment, but one I remembered from decades earlier when, just after sunset, I had found myself on the same verandah leaning on the same railing.

It was a comet.

Yes, yes, I know. Like all celestial bodies, comets are *not* small. But the space they take up in the sky, the solid angle they subtend, *is* small. Should I have held my thumbnail out at arm's length, this thumbnail is the amount of sky it would have taken up. That's the core of the comet, the tail, and all.

I'm sorry. I don't remember the name of this comet. Around this time, the turn of the 20th into the 21st century, there were quite a few of them. Most of them, like Halley's, were underwhelming, mere smudges to the naked eye out there in those mysterious depths to which we, earthbound critters, are unlikely ever to venture.

But this comet was the real deal. It was like nothing else I had ever seen before, and perhaps never will again. And, every evening for about a week, at the same time, it flaunted its spectacular tail for my benefit.

Perhaps one of you good people reading this dispatch of mine saw it too, and can enlighten me apropos its name.

Notwithstanding, name or no, it was a small miracle. The sort of small miracle of which a life well led should be made.

4 May 2023

Voices

How beautiful Australian rivers can be!

This exquisite picture is of the Thompson River in Western Queensland. It's one of those rivers that empties its waters into the Lake Eyre basin in South Australia, the nearest thing we have in Australia to an inland sea.

The closest significant human settlement to where I took this picture is the large town/small city of Longreach, just a few kilometres down the road.

Shall we move in that direction now?

Just past the riverbank campground and associated amenities, we come across a lone eucalyptus tree, whose trunk and main branches have been painted in a vivid shade of blue so bold that its sheen might have been stolen from a volcanic crater lake. Why has the tree been desecrated in such a way?

The story has it that each blue-painted tree commemorates a local farmer who had taken his/her life. Suicides happened quite commonly in the 2010s, during the drought that seemed to go on forever. As you can see from my photograph, the drought *did* come to an end eventually but, for many distraught farmers, who promised themselves they'd stick it out for another year but no longer, it must have seemed like a permanent fixture. Some of them hung themselves in the barn or blew their brains out.

Moving a metaphoric stone's throw south-east along the Landsborough Highway, we duly arrive at Longreach. It is a bustling and apparently prosperous town. These days, it owes some of its prosperity to tourism. Such as Janet and me.

Why wasn't Longreach built on the banks of the Thompson from whence we have just come? So many other towns or cities in Australia *have* been built on river banks, presumably because of the amenity a river offered (perhaps still offers) to trade and the like. Think Echuca, Maitland, Lismore, Brisbane, Burketown.

At this point, the penny should drop for you. Those towns/cities mentioned above, and many others besides, have (notoriously) been devastated at one time or another by that other natural scourge circumstances in Australian are apt to throw up: flood. Drought, flood, drought, flood, drought, flood, and the occasional bush-fire thrown in, but never (it seems) the happy medium. It's legendary that this is the way the cookie is apt to crumble in Oz.

So how was it the good folk of Longreach did the sensible thing and built their village on high ground?

The story goes that the founding fathers of Longreach consulted the aboriginal elders when choosing a site. The aboriginal elders recommended the current site, and the founding fathers took their advice.

Now, we're not talking rocket science here. Where waterways are involved, it's common sense to build on high ground some distance from river banks. Then why did all those other towns/cities get built slap bang on the river banks? Perhaps they didn't consult their first nations' people, or else didn't take their advice. Common sense, it would appear, is not always so very common.

Later this year we, the citizens of Oz, will get to vote in a referendum that will ask all Australians of voting age whether or not they approve of an indigenous Voice to parliament and to its enshrinement in the Constitution.

Most voters, I imagine, would see this Voice as a conduit to petition *by* the first nations' people *to* the wider community. But, couldn't the Voice equally well be a *response to* petition *by* the wider community *to* the first nations' people? After all, any Voice can be either a question or an answer. The people of Longreach, it would appear, asked a question of the aboriginal elders, received an answer from them, and acted on the advice contained in that answer. The outcome was all for the good. I doubt the people of Longreach have any regrets.

When it comes to issues of land management and to the concomitant environmental disasters that poor management may bring, the first nations' people have much accumulated knowledge they can pass on to the rest of us. By 'rest of us', I mean mainly the descendants of white colonists or those who followed in their wake. We, the 'rest of us', have not managed such disasters well at all. Droughts, floods, and bush-fires are things we don't really have a handle on.

Consider. Burke and Wills might have survived had they

listened to and taken the advice of the locals – on what the land had to offer and how they might properly use it – in their final tragic days at Cooper's Creek!

So, though it has not been widely canvassed, the Voice *can* operate in either of two directions, and inevitably for the benefit of both parties. And *will* if we are savvy enough to vote Yes.

A Yes vote is a win-win situation. So, let's be savvy this time round.

13 May 2023

Music? Why?

Music is *the* great perplexity of the ages. It seems not to serve any discernible purpose. It doesn't put food on the table. It doesn't build bridges. It doesn't have wheels, or wings, or rudders. It doesn't play any part in the daily hustle and bustle of the trade or barter of commonplace commodities. It doesn't have words to describe it adequately. What *is* its place in the wider scheme of things? Why *is* it (except for those who are erroneously dubbed tone deaf) a cherished part of our life?

Despite its apparent irrelevance, its enchanted vibrations leak via our ears into our brains, often remaining in our skulls for hours/days/weeks as what we call 'ear-worms'. Ear-worms can be produced by inane ditties, their presence inevitably a source of great irritation to their unwitting victim. Or they can come from music of great profundity. Much of the music of Robert Schumann is a source of ear-worms for me though, I might add, generally in a pleasurable way.

Now, when I invite you to examine 'music' here, I don't mean you should confine yourself to studying the physical structure of the instruments or voices by means of which it is conveyed to those listening. That's more in the realm of physics (or anatomy?) than of music. Most musical instruments, including the human larynx, rely on resonances and the like for their operation. That's where the physics comes in.

Nor do I mean you should study musical notation, including the notion of tempered scales. Such considerations lead you directly into the realm of mathematics.

No. I don't mean the mere mechanics of the music. I mean the *essence* of the music, that quality mysterious ephemeral and (some would say) spiritual, that quality not amenable to study by physics or mathematics, that quality capable of engaging and sometimes entrancing us, that quality remaining after the mechanisms of its production are discounted.

Take an example. My favourite piece of music bar none is the *Diabelli Variations* of Ludwig van Beethoven. When I confine myself to the musical essence of this piece *sans* the mechanics, it will inevitably knock my socks off. There's no physics or mathematics here, just an epiphany that takes me to what feels like another universe entirely. I am overwhelmed, feeling emotions I didn't know existed, swept up into a transcendent world of wonder. Why?

On the assumption that I run the risk of rendering these variations tame by excessive repetition, I make a point of rationing my exposure to them. This is how precious to me this astonishing piece of music is. So far, its effect on me has not diminished over time and, b'Jesus, I have known the piece since the 1980s.

Let's speculate on a rationale behind this 'musical essence'.

Some like to think that, in one way or another, music is a sympathetic and synchronous reflection of our mammalian heartbeat. I'm not convinced. If your heart is thumping away in 3/4 time or similar, then you are in serious trouble. I'd advise you to seek medical advice urgently.

Perhaps music can be regarded as a voyage of discovery, with what is there to be discovered vague or unknowable. (But, as the cliche reminds us, it's the journey that's important not the destination.)

Apropos of 'voyages of discovery', consider those epic efforts made by 15th and 16th century mariners to reach the Indies by (counter-intuitively) travelling west from Europe. The outcome of their efforts would have been in the nature of a lucky dip right from the get-go, especially since it was by no means universally accepted that the world was (roughly speaking) spherical. And the unexpected outcome of their voyage was that they discovered the *West* Indies. As opposed to the *East* Indies, damn it, where the exotic spices they coveted were to be found.

Could a musical voyage of discovery solve *our* mystery – that is to say the mystery of why we're so hooked on this thing called 'music' – in similar fashion to the way Columbus and company came up with *their* solution to a problem of geography? And with equally unexpected result?

Consider another voyage of discovery, i.e. that of the Beagle in the 19th century. This nautical adventure played out in parallel to an intellectual one. Charles Darwin was grappling with the concept of a mind-numbing number (measured in millions or perhaps billions as we now know) of species of earthbound life with few obvious interconnections. Famously, Darwin uncovered a rationale behind this chaotic mystery. Known to us these days as the Theory of Evolution, such theory being one of the cornerstones of modern science, it is spelt out in his seminal publication, *The Origin of Species*.

Could it be that if we were to launch a voyage of discovery among the myriad musical compositions, we might find some unifying principle that explains them? A theory of their evolution? An origin of musical essences?

Now, if you find my flights of fancy too heady for your tastes, please don't read any further. Because I'm about to make another even more outlandish suggestion as to the rationale behind what I have dubbed 'musical essence'.

Currently, I am reading a novel, if you could call it that, by one of my favourite writers, Italo Calvino, whose specialty is flights of fancy. The book I am reading is *The Complete Cosmicomics*. Read it if you dare.

In one chapter, entitled *The Spiral*, Calvino imagines – whimsically as is his wont – life as an ancient mollusc, in an era before sighted creatures had evolved. This mollusc was nothing more than a blob of jelly clinging to a rock by the sea. In response to an amorous exchange, and as a defence against predators, this mollusc secreted a goo that duly hardened into a shell. This shell was ornate in structure, potentially beautiful in both form and colour. I say 'potentially' because its beauty could not be realized unless someone or something was around with eyes to see it. Which was not then the case.

Fast forward a few million years. There is now an abundance of sighted creatures. Eyes are commonplace, if not *de rigueur*. Now the beauty of the shell can be appreciated, whereas before the beauty seemed to have no point.

Do you see where my argument is heading? Are you getting my drift?

Perhaps I'll have to spell it out for you.

I'd like to draw an analogy with Calvino's story. We, creatures of this primitive era in which the 21st century is embedded, have developed an ornate structure (viz. music) whose essence is shrouded in mystery. Perhaps some more highly evolved creatures, creatures slated to come on the scene millions of years hence, will have developed the apparatus (a sixth sense mayhap?) to resolve the mystery. And then all will be explained.

You don't buy this? Never mind. We'll know who's right about this a mere couple of million years into the future. So, hang in there. Preserve yourselves in patience.

And why don't you just listen to the music of your choice while you wait? I'd recommend it.

4 June 2023

Racism as Disease

The disease of racism, like that of melanoma (say), comes to the surface with heart-stopping regularity. And, like melanoma, it will go metastatic if not addressed promptly. Once metastatic, it will be much more difficult to deal with. Words like 'intractable', 'entrenched', and 'incurable' come to mind.

The latest high-profile casualty is, of course, Stan Grant, who has resigned from his position of host of the ABC's Q & A program on TV. But there have been many others before him in public life and, regrettably, more will come after. Remember Adam Goodes?

And, in a form of victim blaming, racism frequently excuses itself at the expense of the hapless victim. The phrase, 'he (or she) should be used to it by now', crops up with such regularity I feel like throwing a brick through the nearest window every time I hear it said. Goodes copped it, and I'm waiting, with anger in my heart, for some white-shoed bigot to use it apropos Grant.

There's an unstated – perhaps taboo – irony here. It's this. No matter how white you'd like to insist your skin is, should you take the trouble to track your forebears – those who have had roots in this country – just a tad back into the mists of past time, there's a fair chance you will find that you – yes, *you, you white bigot* – have indigenous genes in your inherited make-up. The more racist a person's stance is, the more they'll try to deny the reality behind this simple demographic consequence of genetics. To them, it's an unpalatable and unconscionable reality.

We should all make the point of asking ourselves, 'Who do you think you are?', and the answer may not always come back as Irish. Or Norwegian.

Perhaps racism is a form of a mental condition – let's call it a disease – known by psychologists as 'projection'. You fear the demons that your genetic make-up might possibly contain, so you rail against those who by public admission or by obvious skin colour fit the bill.

Doing the rounds in some Twitter-infested circles is another example of this disease of projection. It is the pejorative expression 'Stan Grant's rant', possibly made in reference to Grant's performance in his former role – regrettably cut short – as host of the iconic Q & A program, a program in which a studio audience is invited to direct questions on current issues to a supposedly expert panel. Anybody who has watched this program knows that Stan Grant does *not* rant. He is quietly spoken, almost to a fault. Perhaps the person who coined this alliterative but un-clever phrase is the actual ranter, and he/she is determined to offload their perceived fault onto somebody of whom they feel resentful.

Let me venture a personal opinion. Of all the people who have hosted Q & A since its inception, Stan Grant had been the most able. The way he dealt with difficult people on the panel and in the audience is admirable. He is always firmly in control, but never in an offensive way. Quietly and politely, he brought back politicians determined to push their own barrow to the point under discussion, and defused skillfully such inflammatory comments as might come from the studio audience. I am sorry to see him go, shoved out as he was by bigots and (it appears) by insensitive ABC management.

In time (which has the ability to mitigate the effects of all slings and arrows), I hope we shall see Stan Grant in some other public role. I very much look forward to such an outcome.

Bastards of all stripes, and particularly those infected with the disease of racism, must not be allowed to put good and worthy people down.

22 June 2023

Lucky

Southern Right Whale (Eubalaena australis) mother and calf in shallow protected waters.

A panel, set up for the purpose – one of many such that proliferate, purporting to be authoritative, in the online news media – has recently delivered its verdict on the best beach in the world. Is it somewhere in the Mediterranean? Hawaii, perhaps? Maybe Thailand? Or could it be on the east coast of Australia?

None of these. It is Lucky Bay, near Esperance, in Western Australia.

Long before it had attracted fame, or had even managed to get itself mentioned on maps, I visited Lucky Bay with my partner, Janet. We had traversed the Nullarbor Plain from east to west and, at Norseman, had headed south, looking for the coast, and for somewhere to pitch our tent.

We chanced upon Lucky Bay.

The day was gorgeous, and so was the beach. It was sheltered from the restless Southern Ocean by the bay containing it. Within the bay and near its entrance were a couple of picturesque islands. The sand on the beach was so white, at first sight I thought it must be made of salt. And it squeaked when I walked on it.

Nobody else was about. We had the beach to ourselves for the handful of days we stayed there.

Brand-new public facilities serviced the beach without intruding on it. They included a couple of toilets, a single cold-water shower, and ample space for cooking. What more could we want, especially since these facilities were effectively our own for the duration?

We pitched our tent on nearby dunes, cradled by beach foliage. I pumped up our air-bed, and Janet, who had complained of a bad back, lay down on it to rest her aching bones or whatever. I set things up for our stay: our camping stove – powered by portable propane gas cylinders – collapsible table and chairs, our food boxes. In short, I managed all those mundane tasks of camp-craft essential for pulling off a road trip of the kind on which we had embarked.

We had it made. We had hit the jackpot here at Lucky Bay.

If you look up our heaven-sent destination on Google or some such, you will find these days it is visited by loads of people. And it is supposedly frequented by curious kangaroos, unafraid of people. hese kangaroos have become a talking point, an advertising draw-card, a legend via word-of-mouth. Come to Lucky Bay and cavort with the kangaroos.

In our day and on our date, neither the people nor the kangaroos were in evidence.

Everything ship-shape at our camp site, I wandered down to the beach again. As I said, there was not a kangaroo to be seen. There was not a person to be seen. But, b'Jesus, there was *something* to be seen. And it was big.

Not a hundred metres from me, close by in the water, were two southern right whales, mother and calf. I had seen whales before, both southern right and humpback, but never so close up. Bible black (as Dylan Thomas might have said), and framed by turquoise sea and whiter-than-white sand, this pair was an unexpected and unforgettable sight.

Excited by my find, I ran to tell Janet. Dubious, she followed me down to the beach. When she saw them, she forgot all about her bad back. Screaming with child-like delight, and gripped by a reckless excitement, she stripped down to her underwear, and hurled herself into the water, heading in their direction.

Their reaction?

Mother whale was not impressed. She raised her huge bifurcated tail and slapped it down on the water. Whack! It had an effect comparable to that of a dam burst. She did this several times more. Janet heeded the warning. She stopped in her tracks. This whale was bigger than she was, thirty? forty? fifty? times over.

She came back out of the water. We sat down together on the gleaming sand and watched these wondrous creatures from a safe distance.

Later in the day, we found that the whales had migrated to the other side of the bay, close to the islands. We could scarcely blame them. We could still see them: two black blobs in the water, a couple of kilometres away. Safe from our potential intrusion.

How very privileged we had been. We had seen the whales close up, and had even interacted with them in a sense, even though this interaction was one they could have done without.

Their thoughts might have been along the lines, How dare those pesky pink things on two legs invade the bay in which we habitually shelter!

I'm not sure that whales these days would find Lucky Bay suitable as a refuge. By all reports, the invasion of bipeds – of both the pink and the furry variety – is in full swing. Sadly, their sanctuary has been discovered.

Isn't there a way we could share our world with other species that clearly have a legitimate claim to it?

13 July 2023

Cosmicomics

What a revelatory experience it has been to read this 400 page compendium of ground-breaking vignettes.

Cosmicomics are an invention of Italo Calvino and, fortunately, they have been rendered into English by a suite of excellent translators, and compiled into a volume called *The Complete Cosmicomics*. There is nothing like them in modern literature.

How may one describe something as unique as this volume? Its relationship to the genre of fantasy would have to be that of a bible, a blueprint, a template. In much the same way as Dante's *The Divine Comedy* could be described as a bible blueprint or template for the afterlife, or Shakespeare's collected works could be described as a bible blueprint or template for tragedy, for comedy, and for language itself.

Calvino's *Cosmicomics* are absurd. To say most of them are based loosely on science, would be an understatement. In *Cosmicomics*, science is extrapolated to its ludicrous extremity. Science, as it comes across in *Cosmicomics*, is invariably less than accurate, and willfully so. It's like science fiction on steroids. Sometimes, these *Cosmicomics* invoke superseded science, such as the steady state theory of the universe. Some of them play tricks on the mind of the reader with what is known in mathematical circles as Game Theory.

The word 'play' is apposite here. *Cosmicomics* are always delightfully playful, full of paradox spiced with wry humour, and evocative of wonder. Some of them have a final sentence or paragraph that turns everything that comes before resolutely on its head. Which leads me to ask the rhetorical question, Is Calvino playing games with us (his audience of readers), or is he playing games with us?

Calvino's gender assignment will not please everyone, but his use of it is a source of fascination to me. Eschewing any nod to LGBTQI+ identification, he would have us believe that much of the universe, whether an everyday, a celestial, or a prehistoric manifestation, is either male or female. Solar flares, gametes, molluscs, dinosaurs, and – closer to home perhaps – ordinary human beings facing cosmicomical challenges, have one or other of the two conventional genders, which Calvino is typically careful to specify. In this way, he satirizes ever so gently the literary genre of gender-based romantic relationships. Reference the *menage a trois* suggested in the illustration at the top of this blog. You may need to look closely at it to see all three protagonists.

To what might *Cosmicomics* be compared? *The Hitchhiker's Guide to the Galaxy* springs to my mind. Though Douglas Adams had doubtless read *Cosmicomics*, his expanded *Hitchhiker's Guide* – what he called his 'four part trilogy' – is nothing more than a clever and entertaining poor cousin. *Cosmicomics* is the real deal. It is seminal. *Hitchhiker's Guide* seems like a mildly amusing extension of it.

I loved *Cosmicomics*. Like that other masterpiece by Calvino, *Invisible Cities*, it will stay by my bedside at all times, so that I can dip into it whenever I feel inclined and/or find myself in a bad space.

I endorse Salman Rushdie's comment in the blurb on the back cover of my copy. Rushdie reputably says 'If you have never read *Cosmicomics*, you have before you the most joyful reading experience of your life.'

There's a promise for you. And it comes, I assure you, with a challenge or three.

27 July 2023

Working the Room

From *The Coalface*, June 2023

Bob Katter is an ebullient political animal. A journalist I have known has said that Bob can 'work a room' as adeptly as anybody in the game. He is the independent Member for Kennedy in the Australian Parliament. The Electoral Division of Kennedy is located in northern Queensland. Among other things, it is coal country through and through.

I found his photo, complete with iconic white hat and a jacket of his own design, in the June 2023 edition of a rag called *The*

Coalface, which is distributed free of charge, throughout regions where coal is mined, in venues such as *Hungry Jacks*. The jacket bears the motto 'NO CO2 NO TREE, NO TREE NO ME'. It includes a drawing of a koala wearing a hard hat and sitting in a tree.

It is interesting to see that Katter, among other things, is apparently trying to spruik his credentials as a environmentalist. We may be forgiven for our scepticism. After all, he has been known to say (and I paraphrase here) that greenies are about as welcome in Kennedy as a taipan is in a bedroll.

So, what have we here? Politician, everyman, coal industry enthusiast, tree hugger, bush poet. What a chameleonic quality this man exudes.

Of all his multifarious talents, it's his sympathy for the embattled coal industry that has me most worried. As its name suggests, *The Coalface* is a propagandist outlet for coal interests, which matches the views of the Katter we know all too well. Re-positioning coal mining under the umbrella of environmental preservation, as Katter appears now to be trying to do, is a bold move. Could it, perhaps, be a stroke of genius? Extrapolate the motto on his jacket to the extreme, and you are lead to the conclusion that trees would be nothing more than dusky skeletons if coal wasn't being mined.

But Katter is nothing if not a wily fellow. You won't get him saying out loud that the very existence of trees is dependent on us mining the black stuff. That would potentially expose him to ridicule. After all, trees are what our evolutionary ancestors came down from when they began to inhabit caves. There was no coal mining back then, but trees, we are led to believe, were there in abundance.

And, if that's not enough, take yourself back to the time

immediately preceding the glory days of the industrial revolution. Coal was not burnt then, at least not on a mega scale, but trees were flourishing, and certainly (if the evidence is to be believed) more so than now.

No. Katter is not about to put his *own* head in the noose. But, if other less discerning people are prepared to extrapolate his motto about CO2 and trees beyond the limits of believability, what's not good about that? It could be called 'dog-whistling' or 'working the room'. And isn't that the stock in trade of all politicians?

This way, he can disseminate a lie, without being held personally responsible. It'll be those gullible types with less ability to discern who'll duly cop it in the neck should they dare to stick said neck up. They're the ones who'll be held accountable.

Forget truth. What's the most important duty of a politician? Surely, to get himself/herself re-elected. And if an undiscerning Electorate is prepared to vote you in, that's just how the democratic system works, isn't it?

So, good on you Bob. Work the room for all it's worth. It'll serve you well.

And don't forget your white hat.

17 August 2023

A Five Sigma Event

This is the continent of Antarctica. You can see that the land mass is surrounded, especially in winter, by an expanse of sea ice of comparable extent. It is impossible in winter for ships to push through this sea ice, even if said ship has ice-breaking capabilities. Access, then, is by air only. Antarctica is *not* a hospitable place.

Late in summer, suitably ice-strengthened ships can make it to the land mass in certain places. Early this century, I travelled with Janet on board such a ship – a Russian vessel, named after the poet, *Marina Tsvetaeva* – into the northern reaches of the Ross Ice Shelf. Together with the other paying passengers, I was able to get out and tread the rocky terrain. We hiked to such places as Shackleton's hut, and to the grave of Nicolai Hanson, the first person ever to die on this frigid continent. He died there in 1899.

My experience, unforgettable of course, at times felt dangerous. But I'm glad I did it. All of it. My overall experience left me chock full of indelible memories.

But why do I bother to mention my experiences in Antarctica, significant though they may be to me? Why do I mention the sea ice through which we, at various times, had to push? Plenty of people, these days visit this remote continent whose permanent residents comprise mainly penguins, leopard seals, orcas, and the like. So what's the big deal?

I'll tell you what the deal is. According to the scientists that study these things, the winter sea ice this year has experienced a five sigma event.

Sigma is the eighteenth letter in the Greek alphabet. Scientists and statisticians use its lower case form as a measure – called the standard deviation – of the likelihood of an event occurring. Absolute certainty in science is unattainable. But if an event rates five sigmas or higher, the likelihood of it occurring is near zero, i.e. less than the fraction 0.0000003 (or 1 in 3.5 million). The more sigmas the event rates, the more unlikely the event is.

The recent film *Oppenheimer* postulates a conversation between General Leslie Groves and the eponymous J Robert O, regarding the possibility, then doing the rounds, that if the proposed bomb test at Alamogordo went ahead, it would set off a chain reaction in the atmosphere that would destroy all life on earth.

When Groves asks Oppenheimer to confirm this alarming rumour, Oppenheimer tries to reassure him by saying the chances of this are 'near zero'. Realizing his answer has done little to reassure Groves, he then asks 'What do you want from theory alone?', to which Groves replies 'Zero would be nice.'

That's an important difference between a scientist and a lay person. The zero that Groves wants is impossible. The best Oppenheimer can offer is something in the order of a five sigma rating.

What if a verified five sigma event, despite its having 'near zero' likelihood, is found to have actually occurred? Almost certainly it means that some very significant but underlying effect has not been taken into account.

Consider an example from particle physics. When data from experiments at CERN's large hadron collider was suggestive of a five sigma event, physicists concluded that a massive boson not previously seen (an 800-pound gorilla, no less) must necessarily exist. Peter Higgs had predicted the existence of this boson decades earlier on the basis of theory alone. But now the experimental evidence was in, taking the form of a telltale five sigma event. Shortly before he died, Higgs' judgment was vindicated, and the boson was named after him.

So let's get back to Antarctica and its sea ice. The deficit in winter sea ice this year is a five sigma event. That's the science. So where is the 800-pound gorilla to be found?

The most obvious candidate, perhaps the only candidate, is climate change a.k.a. global warming. The evidence from winter sea ice in Antarctica in 2023 is that there is a 1 in 3.5 million chance that global warming *doesn't* exist. It's odds on that it *does* exist.

I wouldn't fancy a bet against those sort of odds.

And so what? you might ask. Let the Antarctic sea ice melt a little quicker if it must. What does that matter to people living in more northern climes?

This is what matters.

Sea ice, being white in colour, reflects something like 85-90% of sunlight falling on it. Ocean water, on the other hand, is dark, and reflects only about 10%. So, when global warming impinges on this system, it …

… melts more sea ice, decreasing the amount of sunlight reflected, thereby contributing to global warming, which …

… melts more sea ice, decreasing the amount of sunlight reflected, thereby contributing to global warming, which …

… melts more sea ice, decreasing the amount of sunlight reflected, thereby contributing to global warming, which …

Do you see which way things are trending, and where things will end?

The beast you have here is known as a positive feedback loop. Such beasts are typical of explosive chain reactions and other such catastrophic events. The pace of climate change, subject to positive feedback, will in no time at all become exponential. That spells doom for all of us, no matter which clime we inhabit.

The worry is that more and more five sigma events are cropping up around the globe, often associated with positive feedback loops.

We ignore the science at our peril. Some have decided to bash these pesky scientists. They don't like the message they deliver, so they'll shoot the messenger.

But such people can deny the truth till kingdom come, aggressively if that's their wont, until finally that truth catches up to them, to the rest of humanity, and to all living creatures on the planet. It's looking as if only those individuals currently approaching the end of their natural life spans, or those who might perchance come face to face with unnatural deaths in their immediate future, will be spared the horrors of a world disintegrating before their very eyes, a world riven by a succession of five sigma events and positive feedback loops.

We could intervene, of course. That's always been an option for us. But is there time left? And do we have the will?

31 August 2023

The Crested Drummer

The Australian Crested Pigeon

Where we live, far from the noise and confusion of big cities, bird life is in our faces at any moment of the day: the kookaburra, the magpie, the black cockatoo, the pelican, etc. And the crested pigeon, shown above.

This bird is commonplace in eastern Australia and, in contrast to the other species in my list, is typically shy, timid, unobtrusive, and loathe to display itself in public. So, why should I go out of my way to feature such an avian nonentity in words on a page (or on its electronic equivalent).

It's because a particular member of the species that hangs

around our place – let's call him/her Peter/Peta or Pete for short – is choosing to charm us every morning with his/her behavior. Starting at about 7:30 a.m., Pete begins to drum with his/her stubby little beak on a discarded stainless-steel tumbler from a clothes dryer whose shell went to God some months ago. We kept the tumbler because we had been persuaded that somebody someday might want to use it to lay down an *umu* (Maori pit oven) in preparation for a *hangi* (Maori steam cooking).

But now, apparently, it serves as a kettledrum.

Once Pete starts up, there is no stopping him/her. He/she keeps the performance up for at least a couple of hours.

As with a lot of bird behavior, it will likely remain inexplicable to us. Birds, I have found, adhere to an agenda not fully comprehensible to us humans. But we can speculate.

Could it be Pete's form of music making? Or an ingenious mating call? Or a homage to his/her own image reflected in the shiny stainless-steel surface? Or all three? Or none of the above?

Whatever the case, it's keeping Pete happy. And keeping us, his/her accidental audience each morning, delighted.

What Pete has taught me is that there are countless species in this world (including ourselves) all running parallel agendas that, like parallel universes, are all unknowable and unattainable by those not in the loop. We humans should have respect for these other agendas, even if we don't fully understand them. It is not at all clear that our agenda is superior. Where is it so ordained?

Examples abound.

Take one conspicuous example. What are the orcas – in the Mediterranean and elsewhere – up to, for example? Why do they ram our boats? I believe the way to go is to let these amazing creatures keep at it, while making the necessary adjustments to our own behavior. Then sit back and enjoy their performance. It's their agenda after all.

Allow me one further example closer to home. Another avian example. This winter, we have seen swallows in unprecedented numbers, gulps of them I am told, this being the correct collective noun. These tiny birds fling their tiny bodies at a (presumed) task with great enthusiasm and at the speed of light. What are they up to? Sometimes, they are building nests, that much we can know, but at other times we can only guess.

> *A skerrick of life on wing, at breathless clip,*
> *so certain in its zealous and mystery-missioned trip.*

We live in an amazing world, if we only allow ourselves to be amazed.

14 September 2023

Brushes with God and his Crew

From my early years, I have had brushes with the immortal invisible One, so invisible I would maintain as to be non-existent. Such brushes have almost always been through unsolicited intermediaries, earthly intermediaries, lurking in the shadows, always ready to prey on young impressionable minds. These days I would say to these pesky intermediaries, Thanks for nothing. And repair, if you will, to the Hell you preach so much about.

One of them surfaced when my age was only in single digits. Once per week, he would arrive at the primary school I attended (Springvale State School no. 3507), unload his apparatus from the boot of his car, and set it up in the classroom. His apparatus consisted of an easel supporting a rectangular board whose surface was lined with soft felt. On this board he would place cut-out figures, also of felt, which duly stuck to the board. Using these figures as avatars, he would tell stories, ghastly stories by and large, hardly likely to impress us, his young charges. One such story, with its own felt avatar as its centrepiece, was of a naked guy, nailed to a wooden cross. Ugh. I recoiled in a mix of horror and disgust. As you would.

On one of his visits, this timid little man had set up a tableau of avatars consisting of the naked guy, impaled at his ankles and wrists, together with a woman (called Mary Magdalene I believe) a Roman centurian, and many others, making up a cast of six to eight in all. Suddenly, a breeze from an open window nearby, caused the felt figures to ripple. Oh, the little man chortled gleefully, we have moving pictures. He alone managed to see the joke. We thought he was pathetic.

I didn't make the association of any of his stories with the notion of a God, one who created us and the whole world, one who wanted us to worship him, one who insisted in having a say in our future after we died. So, I guess his mission apropos us, was a failure. He just didn't get his intended message across. We saw him merely as a purveyor of horror stories.

When I was aged nine or so, I met IC, whose full name I won't reveal, only his initials. He was a fellow pupil in my fifth grade class, and of about my age. We became very very close friends. It was the first time in my life I had had a real soul mate. It was an invigorating and transformative moment for me.

Whereas most of my classmates were into gross physical activity – dangerous playground games like hoppo bumpo and British bulldog – IC and I played word games in the sand. In class, to the annoyance of our teacher, we would bet on the next word he, the teacher, would utter. IC introduced me to the world of the intellect as an alternative to the quotidian world of rough and tumble. This possibility was new to me, and I embraced its unique possibilities with relish. IC changed my life.

IC and I were inseparable at this time. But there was a catch. One day, he introduced me to God and His associated paraphernalia. IC's father, I believe, was a pastor in some obscure quasi-church in the district, so IC was willing and eager to pass on the Good News to me, including the news about Sin, Hell, and their causal relationship. According to IC, whom I had come to trust implicitly, it was essential that I confess all of my sins to God forthwith, and to ask for His forgiveness if I was to avoid Hell. Since Hell went on forever, and was definitely a place to be avoided, I should (in IC's informed view) take this advice to heart very very seriously.

Around this time, some graphic pictures of Hell emerged in the school environment, presumably from the local Catholic church. They were, I realized much later, Gustav Dore's impressive sketches based on Dante. These stark representations, epitomizing an extremity of horror, put the wind up me big time. Wild horses couldn't have stopped me confessing my sins, which (back then) consisted of really serious stuff like lying, swearing, and disobeying my parents.

My parents? What was their view on the God question? Well frankly, all their time and energy went into putting their lives together again in post-WW2 Australia. For them, thinking – especially about such a thing as God – was a luxury they couldn't afford. Labels such as 'atheist', 'agnostic', or even 'pragmatist' would have been grossly inaccurate if such had been applied to them. Should you want to find a suitable label for them, it would have to be something like 'indifferentist'.

My parents being no help to me when it came to this particular matter, I fell back on IC as my only option. I really really wanted to avoid this place called Hell at all costs.

From this moment on, the 'road of life' for me took a significant turn. It seemed that, at every bend in this road, snake oil sellers from behind every roadside shrub would assail me, all with the same story. The story involved God, Hell, and what they called my Salvation. Their message was, in essence, the same as that I had heard from IC, but I'm sure my soul mate was not directly involved. These Johnnies come lately crossed my path in much the same way as had Dore's sketches, viz. out of the blue. Shills that they were , they must somehow have sensed my vulnerability, post IC, and were coming for me.

I haven't a clue what drove them, but they seemed to have a *modus operandi* or two. They staked out places where young impressionable children were to be found, such as schools, summer holiday venues, etc. Once they got a leg in, they were virtually impossible to dislodge as they set about grooming any children they could lay their hands on. They were legion, pervasive, and ubiquitous. They usually belonged to organizations with respectable sounding names like Inter-School Christian Fellowship and Crusaders.

How dare they! What they did (and continue to to) is child abuse, pure and simple. How dare they!

Whether sexual abuse was part of their repertoire, I can't say for certain. I didn't encounter it personally. But it wouldn't surprise me if it were true. Where-ever there is an imbalance of power between two parties, the ground is demonstrably ripe for sexual abuse. And there *was* such an imbalance at play here.

The jury is out as regards the sexual nature of the abuse they served up. But not on the fact of the abuse *per se*.

These abusers of children, then, made it clear to us quite early on that God expected us, the child 'converts' they made, to pass on the Good News to others at every opportunity presenting itself. To do otherwise was a sin of omission, and we all knew where sins of any stripe would get you in the next life. They could quote chapter and verse to back this up. So, in such manner, they worked to set up giant Ponzi schemes of religious zealotry.

How did they operate on the ground? Let me inform you. Among other things, they ran their own summer camps on the beach, and weekend seminars in the city purporting to help students with difficult subjects like maths and science.

Take the summer camps they ran. Once you were captive to them in this environment, they would conjure up as much camaraderie as could be extracted from the benign setting of sun, sea, and sand. They would arouse your emotions by inviting you to join in singing Wesleyan hymns, always the most stirring ones. They would tell you tall tales about how that naked man nailed to the cross (a.k.a. Jesus the Son of God) had planned it all so as to save you from your sins. They would take you aside in one-to-one 'counseling' sessions just to hammer things home. After that, they would pronounce you 'born again', and insist that you go out into the wider world and spread the Good News.

The same happened on the weekend seminars, except that they would mix in a jot of jolly fun with numbers such as pi, e, and i, just so they couldn't be accused of misrepresentation.

i am embarrassed to admit that I was duped, at least initially, by these people. Like any impressionable child, I was easy prey for them, the sort of prey they chose to seek out. It took me until my late teens to shake off all the sinister baggage they had foisted on me.

From your moment of birth, you must necessarily face a

conundrum. The world you are born into is notoriously difficult to make any sense of, at least initially, and you must figure things out from scratch all by yourself. Thrown in the deep end as you are, it doesn't help to have happy-clapping scoundrels laying trip wires across your path.

Nowadays, thanks largely to a most insightful man called Charles Darwin from the mid 19th century, and to the findings of modern cosmology, I am free of their pernicious philosophy. I have worked out a framework for my life that is majestic in scope, a framework within which I have no trouble working, a framework that has the ring of truth about it. And truth is a wonderful thing. It is truth we all seek, or should seek. For one thing, truth sets us free from those who harbour bad intentions towards us.

Within my framework, death is OK, and Hell doesn't exist. I love the Dore sketches, and I love reading Dante. But these latter are strictly in the realm of imaginative fiction. I am grateful to IC, whom I see as a victim like myself. But I can't abide those charlatans who did their darnedest to sell me (and others like me) a rogue philosophy.

I believe they still thrive to this day and are up to their old tricks. In the interests of new generations of young impressionable minds, I think it is incumbent, on wise men and women with the power to do so, to strive to put a stop to the evil lurks of these unmentionables. They should stamp these parasites out. Cockroaches are more deserving.

23 November 2023

Black

Janet Louise Ward, born 9/9/38 in Oakland, CA, died 28/10/23 in Hakodate, Japan.

My trip to Japan has ended tragically. Janet, my beloved partner of 33+ years, choked on a fragment of food that stuck in her windpipe.

I am beside myself with grief, and not functioning in the real world. There is nothing more I have to say at the moment, except to ask you to hold me in your thoughts.

14 December 2023

Dealing with Extreme Grief

Grief is something with which we all, except for a lucky few, will have to deal sooner or later. Extreme grief, such as I have recently experienced, will come to an unlucky few of us. My recent experience of extreme grief resulted from the accidental and unexpected death of my partner of 33+ years. This, I believe, is about as extreme as grief can get. Perhaps some of the people in Gaza right now are experiencing worse.

Six weeks or more later, I believe I am in a position to analyze rationally the early stages of grief – the stages which I have dubbed 'extreme' – and to give some pointers to anyone unfortunate enough to be similarly afflicted. Be warned. As I have discovered, it won't be easy.

Do you imagine I'm a cold fish for being prepared to analyze my grief like this while I am supposedly still grieving? Believe me, I *am* still grieving . There is no 'supposedly' about it. You really would not want to feel like I feel right now. The act of writing about my grief is actually useful to me. It is cathartic.

Extreme grief has the potential to loosen your anchor to the real world. The anchor will drag, and you will be adrift amid a whole sea of false realities. Your problem now is to become re-anchored to the 'real' reality, before you react precipitously to one of the false realities, thereby making a bad situation worse. You are, in effect, suffering a mini-psychosis at this point.

My advice based on my recent experience is: do nothing at all radical during this period of re-anchoring. Restrain your impulse. If possible, find some routine task to occupy your mind while you are waiting for this to happen through natural healing processes. Which it will. It has (mostly) for me.

The underlying grief will remain. It will likely remain for years, probably for life. But the delusional phase that comes with the extreme form of grief will hopefully be gone. You will now be able to think clearly and plan your life rationally. You will not lose people you thought were friends as a result of precipitate action.

I am not a psychologist. I am not a counsellor. I am just a person who has been through the worst kind of mill and believes he has some useful advice to share. I'm not trying to explain extreme grief to you. That would be an impossible task. Nobody can understand extreme grief unless they have actually been through it.

I hope it never comes your way but, if it does, the tiny scrap of advice I offer here may help you cope.

21 December 2023

Kotsuage

On 31 Oct 2023, my deceased partner, Janet, was cremated in Hakodate, Japan. She had died an unexpected and accidental death three days earlier. My son, John, was with me. I cannot properly describe my feelings at the time, except perhaps to say they were blackest black. I was grief-stricken to an extreme degree not capable of explanation to anyone who has not actually experienced it themselves. I was barely functional. As I described in my last blog (entitled 'Dealing with Extreme Grief') I was not anchored in the real world.

John and I waited at the crematorium for Janet's body to be burnt. The place where we waited was a room comfortable in a cold, clinical, and unadorned way. I seem to remember it had wide windows with views over the beautiful Hakodate harbour. After a couple of hours of waiting, we were invited out, and led to a similar room, but one without windows or view.

Here, waiting for us, was a tray like a hospital guerney, containing smouldering ashes and bones embedded in hot coals still faintly red. Obviously, they were Janet's ashes and bones. The larger bones, including the skull, were still more or less intact and in place. I imagined I could recognize Janet herself in the laid-out bones. The Japanese cremation procedure apparently insists that major bones remain intact for inspection by family.

I was starting to feel horrified, but nothing would prepare me for what came next.

A funeral attendant stepped forward, offering me a pair of chopsticks. It dawned on me that I was being invited to use the chopsticks to transfer the bits of Janet I wanted to keep to a nearby urn. A knuckle bone here. A tooth there. Whatever bit of Janet I chose to transfer to the urn.

This was kotsuage, a Japanese funeral tradition. I believe it is of Shinto provenance.

My reaction to events up until this stage had been passive. But now I felt the call to spontaneous activity. Fight or flight? Flight it would be. I fled from the room faster than Speedy Gonzales would have.

At first, I excused this procedure on the grounds it was Japanese tradition. But later I decided, tradition notwithstanding, it was gross cultural insensitivity with a distinctively Japanese flavour. Later still, I found I could not lay the blame entirely on the Japanese. I felt the Australian Embassy, with whom I had been in contact earlier regarding Janet's death, might have warned me about kotsuage.

They could have headed off an event that distressed me as much as did Janet's death itself.

4 January 2024

My Rescue from Hakodate

Why did I have to be rescued from Hakodate or, more specifically, from the La Jolie Hotel in the district of Motomachi?

I had to be rescued because, in late October of this year, Janet, my partner of 33+ years, died an accidental death there while we were on holiday, and I fell in an almost comatose heap as a consequence.

Hakodate is a very pleasant port city at the southern end of the northernmost island of Hokkaido in Japan. La Jolie is an extremely lovely boutique Hotel in a desirable neighbourhood close to many of the things tourists might want to see. I would go back to Hakodate in a trice, and stay at La Jolie without hesitation. The staff there treated me with grace and courtesy, almost like a friend, even though my partner had just died in their Hotel.

So, with me incapable of any sensible action, I had to be rescued. And, within a day or two, my son (John) had arrived from Melbourne to do just this.

John did a sterling job. He managed to get me out of myself to the extent that this was possible. We dined at some fine restaurants. He started the process of making a claim on my travel insurance. He was with me for all the police reports and talks with funeral people. He was with me at the cremation, when the Japanese custom of kotsuage was sprung on me. See my previous blog for an induction into this most disconcerting tradition.

All preliminary formalities completed, we were able to leave. We began a 36 hour journey from Hakodate in Japan to Perth in Australia. The overnight flight from Haneda (Tokyo) to Sydney was endurable but only just. On arrival in Perth, I was taken under the wing of my daughter (Jenny) and son-in-law (David). Now, almost two months after Janet's death, I'm still living in their spacious home in Mosman Park, a suburb in Perth that would be considered among the most desirable.

Jenny's household consists of Jenny herself, her husband David, and my four Perth grandchildren. It is a medical family. Jenny is head of Cardiology at the massive Joondalup hospital servicing the northern suburbs of Perth. David is, among other things, Professor of Cardiology at Notre Dame University in the southern suburbs. They know, and are known by, most of medical Perth.

My physical health had taken a beating from the shock of Janet's death. For one thing, my balance was shot to pieces. So,

I was promptly taken under the wing of some of Jenny's medical colleagues. Calling in favours, she was able to get my neurological condition checked out thoroughly by the very best people in Perth. Among other things, I was subjected to such pleasures as an MRI scan, and to the testing by electric shock of the condition of my peripheral nerves.

The tests showed my neurological condition was pretty good. There was something else going on here. They found it.

I was being slowly poisoned by a drug prescribed to assist in my recovery from the Poly Myalgia Rheumatica I contracted about a year earlier. The drug was affecting my sense of balance big time and hence my ability to walk. Unfortunately, I'd been taking it for some time, so after I stopped taking it, I didn't get an instant recovery. It took weeks, and my body is still not completely free of the poison.

Meanwhile, my daughter advised that I seek medical attention for my benign but enlarged prostate, a condition from which many men of my age, and even younger, suffer. She advised me to get a TURP (Trans Urethral Re-section of the Prostate) while I was resident here in Perth where class-A medical attention was on hand. So, I'm now lined up for this TURP thing which will presumably happen in January or February. Then, I'll return to my home in Keppel Sands, having had a rest period in which to recover from the unspeakable tragedy that had happened back in October. What's more, and in no way planned by me, I will have been the beneficiary of a first-class medical makeover. OMG. Perhaps I can face the future with a modicum of enthusiasm.

Frankly, I can't wait to get back to Keppel Sands, and to the folk I regard these days as my people. I feel I can now confront the ghosts that will inevitably be waiting for me around every corner, in the house formerly belonging to me and Janet, but now belonging to me alone.

I am really really grateful to those family members – my son, daughter, and son-in law – who rescued me from the impossible situation I faced in Hakodate.

Family that will be there for you when needed are truly a precious commodity.

18 January 2024

Move Fast and Break Things

Move fast? Break things? Was this the motto of Islamic State, from the days when they launched their successful attacks on parts of Syria and Iraq back in 2015, and laid to waste much of the ancient city of Palmyra?

No. It's a motto that came out of Silicon Valley, CA, at more or less the same time.

Its author is purported to be that intellectual giant, Mark Elliot Zuckerberg, founder of Facebook. The motto had been – and remains as such to a large extent – a guiding principle for tech start-ups in the '10s and '20s, until a recent and much-overdue rethink began to take shape, initiated presumably by some among the techies with a modicum of social conscience.

So, might all this fast moving and breaking be dubbed Blitzkrieg? The lightning war of Hitler's regime in Europe in the late 1930s and early 1940s? A cap that fits should always be worn. I suggest the B word would be an apt descriptor in all the instances to which I have alluded, viz. for the Nazi thugs in their advance through France and the low countries (this being, of course, the progenitorial instance of Blitzkrieg), for the IS bandits in Palmyra, and for the Silicon Valley wrecking crew in the tech world.

My reading of the situation as of now is that we, in Australia, are not yet at the rethink stage. The motto is still going gangbusters here, Typically, trends in this part of the world will lag behind trends in the northern hemisphere by months or even years. Halifax. Are we destined always to be the laggards?

What things have been broken in this Silicon Valley blitz? Well, try print newspapers, and the print publishing industry in general. When was the last time you bought a print newspaper? When was the last time you read a decent novel?

But it's in the field of AI (Artificial Intelligence) that the tech rambos threaten to bring about the most spectacular breakage, a breakage which, if successfully accomplished, could threaten the very existence of humankind.

Natural human and other animal intelligence is nuanced by a mysterious something, described variously as 'consciousness', 'self awareness', 'sentience', 'identity', etc. It is that quality enabling each one of us to identify as 'I' and having the requisite feelings to go with such self identification. It is presumed to have arisen through the vague, inexact, and circumlocutory mechanism of human evolution.

The holy grail of AI is considered to be AGI (Artificial General Intelligence) in which this particular nuance is built in alongside intelligence per se. If achieved, AGI would create an intelligent machine calling itself 'I', a version of ourselves that is potentially an improvement on what we are. Our mind, being the product of random evolution, will necessarily be imperfect. The minds of the machines we create, not to mention the machines themselves, should not be so encumbered. They will be a better version of ourselves.

And they will know it!

Given they will be at least as capable as we of making judgment calls, what might we now expect? The details of such are the stuff of science fiction. But, in broad terms, we can assume it won't be pleasant for us. Likely they would choose to exterminate us *en masse* as if we were vermin, which to them we *would* be. This would represent the biggest return of carbon to the environment since the eras when fossil fuels were formed from the decay of plant and animal matter millions of years ago. We might speculate that a lucky few of us might be kept in a zoo for their amusement. And as *their* monument to *our* stupidity.

This is the rosy future research into AGI may have to offer us.

Of course, AGI has not been accomplished, and may never be. There are many skeptics out there (including me) who believe it is unlikely ever to be realized. Some skeptics go further, insisting that the AI bubble as a whole is about to burst. But skeptics have been wrong before. What should worry us is that the end goal of much AI research is AGI. Should AGI turn out to be a go-er, you can bet your bottom dollar the move-fast-and-break-things crowd will press hard for its development. The genii will then be out of the bottle, the masters we have unwittingly created will be in control, and we will be well and truly cactus.

In the interests of ourselves, and of all the delicate and precious things about human life we hold dear, we should not let this happen. Isn't it time for a rethink?

22 February 2024

The Virtue of Quiet Contemplation

Look at this photograph. It is of the Green Mountains in South East Queensland at sunset as seen from our room in O'Reilly's guest house in July 2022. It seems like yesterday.

Does it grab you? Or do you just think 'ho hum'?

At the time I took the photograph, I was mesmerized by what I saw. My eyes were glued. For about an hour or so, I let the scene sink into my inner being. It was a moment of quiet contemplation. No other thoughts, potential or actual, could get a look in. Then, of course, the sun set.

What exactly was I contemplating quietly? Just the nature

of nature really. And how it moves so slowly and inexorably, disregarding the frenetic and chaotic existence we, if unwary, are tempted to make an integral part of our lives. Most people I know, I'm afraid to say, have yielded to this temptation, and are not the better for it.

Woody Allen, wedded as he is to his New York apartment, is reputed to have quipped, 'I am at two with nature.' Looking at the photo above of the scene that so mesmerized me, I find myself pitying the man. Fast motion, fast living, will surely get you somewhere fast, but where exactly? Nature will move slowly, but its destination is identifiable, meaningful, and satisfying.

Forget the latest gadgets. You won't rule them. They will rule you. Put aside an existence totally based on material concerns. Sure, you have to make a living, but why go way way beyond that, as so many people do unthinkingly? Toys for the boys, or pearls for the girls, will ultimately fail to satisfy. You should find yourself a time and a place for quiet contemplation.

And stop trying to keep up with the Joneses. Be true to yourself. Your name is not Jones, unless perhaps it is.

You don't have to go to the Green Mountains precinct. There are many places closer to home for you. The time? You have to set aside the time for it.

Give it a try. I have.

4 April 2024

Tardis or Big Top?

At last I am home, after the journey I'd like to forget, via Hakodate and Perth. From the outside, my home is an unprepossessing low-set cottage in beautiful undiscovered Keppel Sands, complete (you'll note) with colourful wheelie bins.

But go inside, and it's another world entirely.

Like the Tardis, of Dr Who fame, the outside is deceptive. Nothing more than a public telephone box – these days an antique collector's item – the Tardis looks small on the outside. But go inside, and a whole Bunnings store meets the eye.

Likewise my home. The outside is the low-set cottage as per the photograph, surrounded by sheltered decking on all four sides. But get inside, and you're greeted with a sight you never would have expected in your wildest dreams, and that looks far too big to fit inside its frame. It is like a second big bang. A vast universe suddenly appears before your eye.

Specifically, you are immediately confronted with a soaring cathedral ceiling supported by imposing polished wooden beams covering what is mostly an open plan of six rooms. The whole effect takes my breath away even today.

This effect is, holistically, like that of a circus tent, a 'big top', but with extraordinarily solid beams in place of flimsy canvas. The beams radiate out to the perimeter, in a geometric formation that, in its precise configuration brings to mind the ordered structure of crystals or something of similar blueprint. They radiate from two central points supported by wooden poles six or seven metres high. You cannot but feel like a giant in such surroundings. A giant among men (and/or women). Leave low ceilings and the like to dwarfs!

The immensity of the space and its airiness conveys an impression the house is afloat on a benevolent and ambient breeze. This is an illusion. Those laminated beams are bloody heavy. And the poles are anchors striking deep into the ground. This house survived Cyclone Marcia in 2015 with barely a shudder.

The warm colours – the varieties of red and brown – the colours of sunset – colours inevitable in an interior predominantly of wood and wood laminate – delight my senses, embrace me, and make me feel instantly at home. It is the prototypical warm welcome for me. There is not a trace of cold or chill to be found in these benevolent premises.

And on the inside looking out, you have a view through glass and through magnificent greenery to the Pacific Ocean and to multiple coastal islands seemingly afloat on the blue. What more is there to like?

And who designed this amazing house? Janet Ward, my late partner, much loved, who always was a frustrated architect.

I was very much afraid I might encounter ghosts when I returned home from Perth recently. I was dreading the possibility of finding Janet in every nook and cranny of this house. It didn't happen. Certainly, the house itself is one huge ghost, but a ghost that smiles on me. It is a ghost I can live with. It is a ghost I *want* to live with. And I feel it wants to live with me.

These might seem strange and superstitious sentiments coming from a professed atheist. Please cut me some slack. These are feelings I have that, in the course of the daily grind, seem unavoidable – perhaps essential – to me. They are not yet outright beliefs, and may never become such.

But they are a comfort to me in the exceedingly hard times I am experiencing at present. Let me hang on to them for a bit.

11 April 2024
Box of Tricks

Here is a follow up from my last blog. In that blog, I described the house I live in as having an interior that didn't look as if it would fit inside the exterior, rather like the contents of the fictional Tardis wouldn't fit inside Dr Who's magical phone box.

In my blog, I then described the interior in words but, as is said, a picture is worth a thousand words. So, here is the picture.

See what I mean?

The soaring ceilings and the massive structure of exposed beams of the interior don't look as if they could fit inside the modest low-set exterior, whose picture can be seen in my last blog. But they do.

My beloved partner, the late Janet Ward, was a frustrated architect. In her day, only men were supposed competent enough to do such stuff. So, thirty odd years ago, we agreed she should design our house. She did so, and after it was built, we entered for our first look at the finished product. I remember being amazed, among other things, at the Tardis effect.

I imagined she might have said or thought something like '… and now for my next trick …'

It was her last trick I wish she had decided against. This was the trick where she ingested a piece of food into her windpipe, and choked to death. This only happened last October, and I am still in an immense state of shock.

But I live inside the beautiful house she designed and, when I contemplate it, I feel Janet's warm embrace. It is a friendly loving house. It is Janet.

When I scratch around for words to describe my relationship of 33 years and 18 days with Janet, the word 'love' comes to mind. But this word is overused and, in the present context, inadequate. I would say instead that for every day we were together, from first to last, she enthralled me. Without being too presumptuous, I like to think I enthralled her in much the same way.

Now I must leave it to the house to enthrall me.

25 April 2024

The Windorah Experiment

Windorah is a very small town in the amazing channel country of south-west Queensland. Its permanent population, I believe, is about 100. When I approached from Quilpie in August 2022 across the red dirt, I came across the unexpected view in the photo above. It looks derelict, and it is. Since my visit, I understand it has been dismantled totally.

But what was it?

The parabolic dishes, rusty though they are in this photo, would once have been gleaming bright as, tracking the sun, they concentrated its rays towards their central collectors. These collectors would, as a consequence, have become very hot, as anybody knows who has started, or tried to start, a fire using a magnifying glass.

Heat is not the most versatile form of energy, so a tailored physical process of some sort, otherwise known as an 'engine', would have been used to convert heat to electricity. Electrical energy is an extremely versatile form of energy, as anybody – like me – who runs a household on electricity knows.

The idea, as envisaged by Ergon Energy and the Queensland Government, would have been to provide Windorah with a source of power independent of the grid or of diesel generators. It was a bold experiment. It might have been a prototype for small and remote communities round Queensland. But it evidently failed.

What went wrong?

Perhaps the problem was getting spare parts, repair kits, and skilled technicians to such an isolated part of the country. Perhaps there were too many moving parts that could go wrong. Perhaps the more direct science of photovoltaics – whose icon is the ubiquitous rooftop solar panel – caught up with it. Perhaps it was all of the above.

I used the F-word a few paragraphs ago. Failed. But was the Windorah experiment really a failure?

Any successful innovation is the end result of a series of failures. Failure is the mechanism through which technological advance becomes possible. Failure is an excellent teacher. *That* one failed, but perhaps *this* one might work. Let's give it a go.

I believe Ergon Energy and the Queensland Government are taking this approach. They are planning other solar projects in several regional precincts, including Windorah, based this time on photovoltaics.

They should be commended.

9 May 2024

The Scattering of Ashes

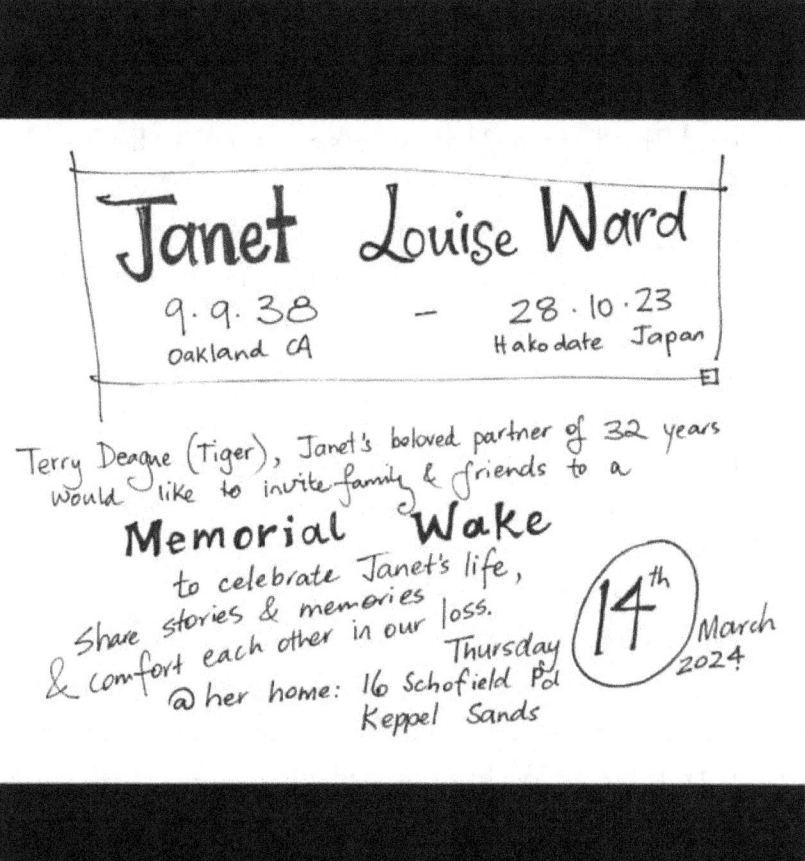

I doubt scattering of ashes is practiced much in Japan, which is where Janet died. It seems inconsistent with the Japanese funereal practice of Kotsuage, a practice which lends itself more towards the keeping of an urn in a dedicated family crypt. Having had the misfortune to experience Kotsuage first hand, I have portrayed it in one of my earlier blogs as a bizarre in-your-face ritual inimical to Western sensibilities.

Japan aside, the scattering of ashes is certainly widely practiced in Australia.

The idea behind ashes scattering, I imagine, is that the beloved person who has died shall have their ashes returned to the natural environment, preferably to a particular part of that environment they loved. That happened with Janet's ashes on 14 March of this year (2024) in a ceremony attended by some of the Keppel Sands locals, some people from Rockhampton, and even some from New South Wales and Victoria. It was a small, but representative group of people Janet loved, or at least chose to associate with.

The invitation in the photo above was designed by one of my neighbours with an artistic bent. She made one slight mistake, for which I shall forgive her. Janet was my beloved partner for thirty-three years and eighteen days. We met on 10 October 1990, a Wednesday. A magical day for me and, I believe, for her too. Words cannot express how much I miss her now.

So, on 14 March 2024, those who would participate in the ashes scattering, numbering around thirty, gathered on my front verandah. The weather was perfect for the occasion: fine and mild with a gentle breeze. We had expected rain.

My mind was in a strange place, which was to be expected given this was in some respects the culmination of all the trauma I'd been through over the past months. Moreover, I'd never participated, let alone been the principal, in an event such as this. Sausage rolls and other items of finger food were served by a wonderful young local woman, Amy, who had tattoos over most of her body and a heart of gold. I just went with the flow. After stories had been told, we set off, me leading and carrying the urn, to a place overlooking a small but beautiful beach with gently lapping waves. Balm for the eyes and music for the ears.

Janet had asked that, in the event of her death, her ashes should be scattered from the *top* of the headland (Musa Head) overlooking this beach. We compromised. Many of the people assembled would not have been capable of ascending the headland. B'Jesus, one was dragging an oxygen cylinder behind him to assist his breathing. So the scattering took place at the *bottom* of the headland.

Janet had also asked that *Kol Nidrei* be played during the scattering, this being one of her favourite pieces of music. I had some sort of amplifying device attached to my mobile phone, and it worked a treat. Music filled the air as I spread the deathly white ashes over green foliage. Janet would have been impressed.

Stop there.

She *was* impressed. I swear she was present at that moment, a moment hanging in suspension according to some fortuitous dispensation from the laws of physics. I could feel her fingers gently caressing the palm of my hand and could smell her warm breath in the air we co-inhabited with such mutual delight, as we had in life.

Sorry, she said.

What for? I asked.

Leaving you alone so abruptly, she said.

But you did keep me enthralled for thirty-three odd years, I said.

Thirty-three years and eighteen days, she said.

This was, indeed, a strange, almost mystical moment for me and in more ways than one. What struck me, as I took in the scene before me, was how those assembled formed an almost perfect circle with me at one far point on the perimeter. To me, it felt like we were participating in some pagan (Celtic?) ritual, wondering when the human sacrifices would perhaps be called for. Why did they adopt this regular formation so spontaneously? Why did they not just mill around me like a scraggly flock of goats waiting to be fed?

From that point on, only anti-climax could follow. The ashes had been scattered. The job was done. Some people went on their way, while others gathered back at my verandah to talk whatever shop took their fancy: the marketplace, the office, the factory floor, the racecourse, the tennis court.

When a loved one dies, in the process leaving us bereft and laying us low, a ghastly and oh so sad mysticism hijacks the core of our being. But mundane life lurks assiduously in the background, a bully-boy insisting we re-engage with its everyday concerns.

This is the way of the world, and is perhaps a necessary evil.

Afterword

I was somewhat surprised to find, on my completion of this compilation, that the whole deal has a well-defined narrative thread running through it, literally from go to woe. It traces my progression from a person who felt confident he could mould his future as if it were modeling clay, to a completely different person – ill-defined as of now – who has much more respect for the input to his future made by intractable life events outside of his control. Events of profound tragedy are in this category, and will – I contend – exert a profound effect on whoever is unfortunate enough to find themselves in collision with them.

So, I am 'born-again' as the fundamentalist Christians would say, but not at all in the way these pesky God-botherers would have it. I am a new person, but not one of their pestilential stripe.

Should you want to see the continuation of this narrative thread, it is and shall be covered by the blogs I have posted and shall post subsequently on my webpage (**https://terrydeague.com**). Or you can get them delivered to your inbox by subscribing to my newsletter.

Wish me luck in my daunting new journey. I appreciate your thoughts, but your prayers are yours to keep to yourself.

Acknowledgements

Thank you, Edwina Mullany, for the wonderful cover illustration, and for the illustration accompanying the very last blog in my compilation, the one dealing with the ceremony held to commemorate Janet's life by scattering her ashes.

Thank you, Sylvie Blair of BookPod, for giving me the opportunity yet again to publish my modest scribblings independently of mainstream publishers.

Thank you, all those people who propped me up in the difficult times that beset me following the death of my beloved Janet, and helped me to find for myself a new way forward, a Life After Janet. Without you, this compilation would not have happened.

And thank you Janet, though you're likely out of earshot, for scarcely batting an eyelid when I took time out to do my own thing, i.e. to write blogs and novels. You, my love, respected the time and space I needed. You were the anchor I needed in all my life's dealings, and I only hope I was able to reciprocate in kind.

About the Author

The author's main paper qualification is a PhD in photonuclear physics, i.e. nuclear reactions induced by photons, from the University of Melbourne. He has necessarily written a number of scientific papers in this field.

In the 1970s, he wrote a review paper on the subject of Global Atmospheric Consequences of the Combustion of Fossil Fuels, which (as might be imagined) was ground breaking at the time.

His literary accomplishments are a short story published in the Australian literary journal *Tabloid Story* in the 1970s, a screenplay funded by Film Victoria in the 1980s but never produced, and two novels, *Where Pademelons Play* (2018) and *The Spaceman* (2021).

Love, Death, the Cosmos, and the Kitchen Sink, an anthology of his blogs, is his third literary accomplishment.